Changing Lives, Changing Societies
ICA's Experience in Nepal and in the World

Edited by
Tatwa P. Timsina, PhD
Dasarath Neupane

ICA Nepal

Changing Lives, Changing Societies
ICA's Experience in Nepal and in the World

Published in October, 2012 by ICA Nepal

Printed in Kathmandu, Nepal

Library of Congress Cataloging-in-Publication Data
Changing Lives, Changing Societies - ICA's Experience in Nepal and in the World/edited by Dr. Tatwa P. Timsina and Dasarath Neupane

Contents

Preface

Acronyms

Case Studies

Fertig-Dykes
3.	Working with Organisations, Malaysia – Ann Epps
4.	Building Civil Society in Far Western Regional of Nepal – Tatwa P. Timsina
5.	Leadership Training in Peru – Ken Hamje
6.	Participatory Project Prioritisation, Afghanistan – Alisa Oyler
7.	Tohoku Earthquake and Tsunami Recovery Projects – Shizuyo Sato
8.	Human Capacity Building through Social Artistry – Tatwa P. Timsina
9.	Responsibility for Sustainability – Radha Subedi

Acronyms

ABCD	Asset Based Community Development
CNT	Centre for Neighbourhood Technology
CMPP	Cooperative Members Participation Programme
CSI	Civil Society Index
CSO	Civil Society Organisation
DNA	Deoxyribo Nucleic Acid
DTAHA	Decentralised Transformative Approaches to HIV and AIDS
GFM	Group Facilitation Method
GDP	Gross Domestic Product
HDP	Human Development Project
HIV/AIDS	Human Immunodeficiency Virus/Acquired Immuno Deficiency Syndrome
ICA	Institute of Cultural Affairs
INGO	International Non Governmental Organisation
IERD	International Exposition of Rural Development
ITHD	Institute of Training and Human Development
JHF	Jean Houston Foundation
LENS	Leadership Effectiveness and New Strategies
MDGs	Millennium Development Goals
NGO	Non Governmental Organisation
PELP	Participatory Leaders Training Programme (translated from Spanish)
PRA	Participatory Rural Appraisal
PSP	Participatory Strategic Planning
SA	Social Artistry
ToP	Technology of Participation
UN	United Nations
UNDP	United Nations Development Programme
VDC	Village Development Committee

Preface

Started in Chicago, USA in 1963, The Institute of Cultural Affairs was developed as a pioneering research organization as the initial laboratory for the development of human capacity building methods and approaches. It started its work taking the "5th City" community on Chicago's West Side as an initial laboratory. From there, this work extended globally, with international offices and projects established starting in 1968.

The Institute of Cultural Affairs International is a global network of national member organizations located in various countries from all over the continents. It has played an active role in transforming the dilapidating economies particularly after the Second World War in Asia and Europe towards prosperity.

Though established quite late, ICA Nepal is emerged as one of the leading NGOs in Nepal. Since its inception, it has carried out massive development activities transforming thousands of lives in Nepal. ICA Nepal, since its inception has always been guided by the principles and philosophies of ICA International. This has led ICA Nepal to take many challenges enabling it to involve in diverse developmental activities.

This book summarizes the opinions and experiences of people involved in ICA through various developmental activities. It explains the role of ICAs in global development. It elucidates various activities developed and implemented by ICAs in transforming deprived communities all over the world. The book has covered the 50 years' of global human development from the perspective of its own involvement. It covers issues such as how we can bring changes in the local area. The book has elucidated overarching role of facilitators in community development. It relies on the premises that human development activities are possible if they are dealt with human ingenuity and skill.

The book covers issues such as the role of leadership on individual, organizational and community transformation. It emphasizes on the need of empowered individuals on bringing changes in the society. The book has mentioned the role of facilitative skills on managing conflict to carrying out research in a participatory way. It has covered several examples of application of facilitative skills. The book has also included case examples of applications of participatory approaches in education, from basic to tertiary level.

The book is very much inspired by the logo of ICA itself, called a "wedge-blade". It represents the work of The Institute of Cultural Affairs guiding all the aspiring ICAs globally. Two halves of the circle symbolizes history and the future, with the line at the centre representing where we stand now – the present. It drives us towards bright future with hope and expectation for better living.

Many authors and facilitators who have spent most part of their life in ICAs have contributed for this book too. This book is the result of their decades of experiences of working in the community from local to national level. The book is the testimony of experienced people belonging to ICAs covering almost a half century of experiences. The book could be a handbook of memoir of human soul who have spent almost whole of their life in bringing change in life and societies or as a guiding companion for the people who would like to work in the community by applying participatory tools and techniques at local to national level.

Global Human Development: 50 Years of ICA's Experience

Bill Staples

S ince the early 60s, the work and growth of ICA has fascinated several generations of thinkers, activists, leaders of social movements and people in every walk of life. Its ability to stay true to its roots in human development and at the same time transform itself according to time and place is of constant amazement to those outside the organization as well as within. The small group of families in the early 60s who originally felt compelled to provide a special service to the world has grown exponentially, with a powerful legacy in almost every nation and in profession. There is an intention and spirit that is carried in the DNA of the organization and it seems as if all those who join consciously in its activities carry the authenticity of the entire organization within them.

Christian Faith and Life Community

In the late 1950s Joseph Wesley Mathews and a small group at the University of Texas studied the practical meaning of social responsibility and linked the actions of individuals to the urgent needs of 20th century, post-war society. They carried the idea of "social pioneer" to Illinois in 1962 and energized the Ecumenical Institute by moving the staff and living communally in an abandoned seminary on Chicago's West Side. This was the beginning of an urban experiment in community reformulation in which "service to the world" was grounded again and again by daily examples of commitment and human expenditure. Theory and curriculum became fused with service and practical action as staff, volunteers, community leaders and citizens all learned from and mentored one another in the hot crucible of 5th City, a decisional community in those several blocks surrounding the Institute.

Iron Man of 5th City

From the mid 1960s hundreds of staff and volunteers worked with the residents of Fifth City developing and testing the philosophy and values of human empowerment along with the practical principles and tools of community development. All of these were severely tested during riots in

1968 which were sparked in neighbourhoods across the United States by the assassination of Martin Luther King. The resolve of community, staff and volunteers to stand resolute in the midst of adversity became a central self-image. Imaginal Education theory and practice was developed and tested during this time, underscoring the important link between self-image and personal behaviour which is still core to ICA and ToP® human development.

When Iron Men
Tune: When the Saints Go Marching In.

When Iron Men go marching in,
When Iron Men go marching in,
There'll be new day tomorrow,
When Iron Men go marching in.

When City Five has come alive,
When City Five has come alive,
There'll be a new day tomorrow,
When City Five has come alive.

Oh when the trend begins to bend
Oh when the trend begins to bend
There'll be a new day tomorrow
When the trend begins to bend.

When the world picks up the sign
When the world picks up the sign
There'll be a new day tomorrow,
When the world picks up the sign.

For Iron Men it's never done,
For Iron Men its never done.
There'll be a new day tomorrow,
For Iron Men it's never done.

For Iron Men it's just begun, ...

Primal Community Experiment

In the early 70s church congregations existed in every community in well over half of the world's countries, providing opportune locations to expand and practice community reformulation on a massive. Large numbers of personal empowerment courses called Religious Studies, Cultural Studies and International Training Institutes were scheduled in 30 countries to awaken thousands of people to global needs and to their own potential. Local groups and committees were set up, primarily in urban congregations and neighbourhoods, to engage people in research, development and task forces on cultural renewal, political awareness, economic revitalization and other topics of local concern. The organization of local cadres and regional councils led to the development of methods of actuation including tactical thinking and implementation, both of which were highly participatory and consistent with the earlier foundations of philosophy, values and imaginal education.

Global research assemblies each summer in Chicago debriefed and reoriented the plans of 50 offices, each one an intentional community rooted in a neighbourhood. Social change theory and analytic screens were studied and developed culminating in the creation of The Social Process triangle, a powerful whole system diagnostic, analysis and change tool that could be applied at the global, regional and local level. Personal and group reflective practices were in constant use by staff, volunteers and neighbourhood program teams leading to refinements in previous imaginal and spirit methods like curriculum design and the focused conversation method, and to new social methods like geo-social, trend, pressure point and contradictional analyses.

When You Are Aware

Tune: When You Are In Love

When you are aware, the whole world is a mountain of care.
Skies constantly weep, over all of the tragedy there.
Then your life belongs to each suffering one everywhere.
When you are aware the whole world is a mountain of care.

Bearing the weight of the world, and the dread of its crushing demands,
Joyously burdened to know that there's no other world on your hands, and,
Your heart start to soar, with the wonder that's filling the air,
When you are aware, the whole world is a mountain of care.

Global Campaigns

Throughout the seventies invitations from many communities lead to the formation of national Institutes of Cultural Affairs, registered charities set up in over 30 countries. Each ICA was aligned with two major campaigns, the global community forum or Town Meeting TM campaign and the global social demonstration or Human Development Project HDP campaign. Town Meetings would blanket a national province or state with one day civic meetings, motivating large numbers of citizens to create long range visions, develop practical proposals and celebrate local culture. From 1975-80 about 10,000 community forums or Town Meetings were held around the world resulting in practical local and regional initiatives, many of which ICA could never hope to support, and a very large network of colleagues and supporters.

The Human Development Projects trained teams of community development practitioners to live and work in specific communities and supported them in implementing whatever catalytic projects the community planned. Each HDP demonstrated the impact and change possible when a small but committed group of people made a decision together. The original 5th City reformulation in Chicago catalyzed Human Development Projects in 24 new locations, one in every time zone, and each of these sparked development in many other communities. From 1977-1981 large scale replication occurred in India, Kenya, Philippines, and Indonesia.

The global campaigns were centralized and intense, with large-scale research, training, fundraising, and interchange functions. ICA developed highly effective approaches for planning and for working together including a community consultation methodology, a community forum method and a participatory strategic planning process. Living Effectively in the New Society (LENS) became a participatory strategic planning process that forms the basis of ToP® methodology. Many of the several thousand ICA staff and volunteers of these global campaigns on eight continents eventually went on to become experts in their specialized fields, leaders of NGOs, organizations and communities, or independent consultants.

The Victory Song

Tune: The French Military Marching Song

If you would a winner be in making trends reality,
Join the surging local will to build the new community.
We can seize the victory, awakening and engaging all;

Across this land the future calls,
To meet the challenge of the day in determining the way,
And with Town Meeting we'll become this history.

If you would a winner be in making trends reality,
Serve the hope of everyone to shape a new society.
We can build a unity where all the earth belongs to all;
Across this world the future calls,
To meet the challenge of our day in determining the way,
And with Town Meeting we'll fulfill this destiny.

Sharing Approaches That Work

By the early 1980s the size and scope of the diverse projects in operation in 34 nations had become extremely complex with health, education, farming, housing, industrial, cultural and many other initiatives. Most ICAs were beginning to document the results of their own community reformulation work but quickly uncovered a plethora of other local development projects that were destined to die in isolation unless a bright light was shone on them. This resulted in the large-scale, global documentation of thousands of community and rural transformation initiatives leading to the 1984 International Exposition of Rural Development (IERD) in New Delhi, and the publication of three volumes of *Sharing Approaches That Work*. This was an appreciative inquiry into all types of community development on a mass scale and the distillation of acceleration factors and suddenly put ICA on a world stage, especially at the level of the United Nations.

At the same time every national ICA was struggling to support its own local operation. The LENS strategic planning process became an important tool for organizational self-support as ICA staff began to find a ready market for participatory strategic planning within corporations, municipalities, governments and not-for profits. It was starting to become common knowledge in society that plans made only at the top stayed only on the shelf, but that plans made by everyone were supported by everyone.

With large scale project documentation complete, UN Economic and Social Commission consultative status accorded, and a marketable and effective planning methodology in hand, all ICAs were beginning to see a new and exciting horizon.

Stories Of New Life
Tune: Starry, Starry Night/Vincent)

SHARING APPROACHES THAT WORK

Stories of new life,
Of people who have willed to do
Together what creates anew
In villages so visions can come true.

Stories of new life,
Fallow fields come into bloom,
Endeavours out of brick and loom
Raise up the poor from centuries' heavy gloom.

Chorus:
    The stories must be told,
    New signs for all the world to see;
    From the pains of hard-won victory
    The future's breaking free.
    We're given back our life in many ways
    And grateful for these days.

Stories of new life,
In summer's rain and winter's snow
The working faces beam and glow,
Prepare the road for those they'll never know.

Stories of new life,
A painted wall with rising sun
Where healthy child learn and run,
Clear water flowing — hope and selfhood won.

National Autonomy

By the mid to late 80s it was becoming apparent that the common ICA philosophy, values and principles of local empowerment and unlimited human potential were more important to staff and volunteers than were centralized institutional programs. Volunteers in many nations were imbedding those principles deeply into the organizations or communities in which they worked. ICA staff used the same principles in all the programs they developed. The first ICA book for general consumption,

Winning Through Participation, was quickly followed by other books and by a magazine of leading edge thinking. Attention was given to codifying and disseminating ICA intellectual property in written form, capturing ICA methods and approaches in books, training manuals, videos and curricula so that they could be shared both inside and outside the organization. Each national ICA explored and pushed its own leading edge, generally in the fields of development, education, economic and planetary unity, or DEEP initiatives.

In this midst of this new national autonomy ICA International was created in Brussels as a communication device for ICAs. UN consultative status, conferred especially for ICA's work in Kenya during the UN Decade for Women, was a symbol of the importance of the continuing programmatic work that was taking place in neighbourhoods, cities, regions and with all types of industries, professional groups, and associations. The Deputy Director of the UNFPA referred to ICA as "The People of the Question" a clear reference to ICA's participatory and facilitative philosophy.

Kawangware, A Sign

Tune: Malalika

Kawangware, a sign of hope to the world.
Kawangware, setting forth in the stillness.
A full past deep in greatness,
Now a time of resurgence.
People working in community
Hear a voice calling those who care.
A place of struggle that creates anew,
Place of glory for all Mankind.
Kawangware, a sign of hope to the world.

Technology of Participation

Throughout much of the 1990s ICA took a leading role in the development of the newly forming profession of facilitation. ICA staff and volunteers on seven continents collaboratively organized regional, national and international conferences on facilitation, and often provided the leadership. The Technology of Participation (ToP®) became the brand name for many of ICA's participatory methods and ToP® courses and training spread rapidly around the world. By the end of the 20th Century an estimated 50,000 people had taken ToP® training, and thousands of ToP-trained facilitators were promoting and leading the practice of participatory decision-making throughout society in a dozen languages and in forty countries, even the former Eastern Bloc countries and China.

Many of the transformational elements of ICAs work over four decades had become condensed and crystallized into the powerful suite of ToP® facilitation methods and tools. The procedures and practices of every part of every ToP® method could be traced back to the values, principles and philosophy of the early Faith and Life Community, the Ecumenical Institute and The Institute of Cultural Affairs. Large numbers of consultants and facilitators took ToP® training explicitly to focus groups to work together. Others used ToP® and a variety of ICA methods more implicitly, to nudge or even transform social systems towards life-affirming human development outcomes, such as environmental sustainability in Taiwanese companies, client-centred care in Canadian health institutions, or staff diversity in UK organizations.

Local Global Program Networks

Throughout the first decade of the second millennium ICA has taken a leadership role in addressing national or regional needs. This has been done by systematically launching local initiatives that demonstrate a focus on a national priority, and then networking the local initiative out to the continental and global level. Each ICA has a solid programmatic thrust within its own nation, and is respected for its programs. But while at first glance it appears as if each ICA is operating separately there is, in fact, a networking of programs continentally and globally, driven by the common global philosophy, values and methodology.

ICA Japan, for instance, is using its private sector and government contacts from the 1980s and 90s throughout Japan to fund dozens of regional and community development initiatives in 20 countries on three continents, and many of these are with other ICAs. ICA USA's large number of ToP Trainers with their extensive network of international contacts have provided opportunities for leadership development through their IToPToT or international ToP training of trainers program. ICA UK has oriented and sent British volunteers to several nations in Africa to work on various on HIV Aids and other initiatives. ICA Canada funded similar program in Africa. ICA Australia has been involved in many projects in South and Southeast Asia. The ICAs in UK, Spain, Germany, Netherlands, Belgium and Bosnia Herzegovina have been regularly networking to assist each other in initiatives throughout Europe. ICAs in Egypt, Kenya, Tanzania, South Africa, Benin, Cote d'Ivoire, Cameroon, Ghana, Zambia and Zimbabwe have all organized efforts among themselves and with other ICA's on programs related to HIV AIDS, reforestation, and women's microcredit. ICA Taiwan and LENS International in Malaysia, with their extensive work in the private sector, regularly provide training opportunities in several southeast Asian countries. ICA Guatemala hosted an ICA Global Conference and several Spanish speaking ICAs with experience in earthquake zones network regularly. ICA India, ICA Bangladesh and ICA Nepal play constant host to other ICAs and regularly share their work on large scale human development.

It is not difficult to see the impact that ICA is still having on its original mission of exploding every person's imagination about their responsibility for the world and their potential service to the world. Just as each person could easily limit their responsibility to their own front door, each ICA could easily use its full time and potential within its own national boundaries. But the DNA of all of us is encoded to be a planetary citizen, or at least a global one, and to hold out the promise of living a fulfilled life to every human being.

Free to Decide
    Tune: Hi, Ho Nobody Home
    (Best sung as a round)

    Free, free, free to decide
    What this world is going to be;
    This imperative is ours
    To be free, free . . . (Repeat)

Transformative Leadership for Sustainable Human Development

Robertson Work

Introduction

The aim of this chapter is to provide a reflection on the critical times in which we live and future scenarios of development, governance and leadership. First a brief reflection is offered on social philosophy and the social contract raising a few important questions. Next the chapter provides an analysis of the critical decade of crisis and opportunity in which we find ourselves, the new civilization that is emerging and the importance of working at the community level. Following this, there is a discussion of the role of transformational leadership in 21st century public service. Finally, the chapter provides a few thoughts on the integration of four key themes and possible actions.

I. Social Philosophy

What is a *human* being? What is development? What then is human development? What is the purpose of societal organization and governance in relation to human development?

These are not only philosophical questions but urgent, practical questions. These are some of the profound questions facing us as a species. Our responses to these questions, both in our individual thought and behaviour and in our collective culture and systems, will determine how human society and life itself flourishes or declines on planet Earth. If this is so, how is it so?

There are many views of what constitutes a human being. Is a human being a spiritual being of infinite worth? Or primarily a consumer of goods and services? Or a resource for economic production? Or primarily a citizen of the State? Or simply another mammal? Or a child of God? Is a human being basically good? Or fundamentally evil? Does each human being who is born have universal rights guaranteed by society? What are the rights of future generations? What is the full potential of each human being? What is the ultimate purpose of human beings on planet Earth or in the universe as a whole? Our answers to these questions spring from our own acculturation and socialization as provided by our culture, religion, political ideology, personal reflection, age, sex, and so forth. Some people believe that only their group is truly human and that all others lack truth and legitimacy.

The dominant answer in the world today to the question of what constitutes development is material and economic progress, industrialization and modernization. The race is on to increase GDP per capita and fuel a consumption-production society at any cost to nature and people. However, this purely economic definition is doing much harm to natural systems and human culture.

Each definition of humanness carries with it an implicit or explicit definition of development. If a human being is primarily a spiritual being, then society would be designed in a way that would help each person realize his/her spiritual potential. If a human being is primarily a consumer, then he/she is to be manipulated by advertisements to purchase certain goods and services. If a human being is primarily a citizen of a democratic state, then she/he is empowered to express her/his opinions through voting and is responsible to act in accord with the laws of the State. If a human being is understood simply as another mammal, then she/he will be treated that way. If a human being is understood to be a child of God, then she/he will be cherished as a holy being.

If a human being is understood to be basically good, then society structures itself in order to nurture this quality and will design systems based on trust of this basic goodness. If a human being is understood as fundamentally evil, then society will design systems that seek to control and punish these dark impulses. If every human being who is born has universal human rights, then society will design systems to ensure adequate opportunities and access to quality education, healthcare, housing, credit and self expression of each and every person. If future generations have the same rights as the present generation, then society will ensure that the resources of the Earth are preserved and developed with this in mind. If every human being has the right to realize his/her full potential in this life, then society will be designed to ensure that this can happen. If human beings believe that they have an ultimate purpose on planet Earth and in the universe as a whole, then this will provoke profound dialogue in society and help direct the design of social systems toward a learning society.

What then is "human development"? As we have seen, different definitions will flow from different views of the human being. In the view of the United Nations and the international community at large, the human being is guaranteed universal rights by society as articulated in the Declaration of Human Rights. The UN has been analyzing and promoting "human development" or "sustainable human development" over the past twenty years. Furthermore, the Millennium Development Goals were agreed upon to provide tangible targets for human development over the short term.

How then do nations and local communities understand the *social compact* that guides the design of social systems for the benefit of all human beings, all living beings and the finite resources of planet Earth including plants, animals, water, soil and air? Based on the Universal Declaration of Human Rights, the social compact directs that human beings agree to care for each other to ensure that each person has the necessary conditions for a full and meaningful life while ensuring that future generations have the same right.

This means that in order for all people to enjoy these rights, no group of individuals should be allowed to make this impossible by the over accumulation of economic wealth, political power or cultural dominance.

With this reflection as a backdrop, what are the current challenges facing humanity and indeed all life on Earth?

II. The Critical Decade: Crisis and Opportunity

Many social analysts, the author included, believe that we have just entered **the most critical decade** in human history – a time to do what is needful or face the direst of consequences. Other generations thought they were it; they were wrong; this is it. If we do the right things, the future of life on Earth can be brighter than we can imagine. If we don't, the future could be dismal and even disastrous.

We are in the midst of a whole systems transformation – a time of chaos, crisis and possibility. We are facing multiple, interlocking crises including climate chaos, economic injustice, increasing poverty, dysfunctional governance, unsustainable energy, gender inequality and an HIV/AIDS pandemic. Each of these crises, however, is also an unparalleled opportunity for reinvention of the human enterprise.

We as a global society have the tools and technology needed to solve each of these crises; what we lack is collective agreement and action. We must, at the same time, transform individual consciousness and behavior and collective culture and systems.

These crises are an opportunity to reinvent nothing less than human society itself from the bottom up, the top down and the inside out based on principles of *sustainability, equity, justice and participation.* We can literally create a world that works for everyone – societies that enable each person to realize her or his full potential.

There are a number of interlocking crises which represent incredible opportunities:

Environmental

The natural systems of Earth that have supported human civilization for the past 12,000 years are changing drastically and human societies must adjust quickly or adapt to a diminished Earth over the long term. Global climate change is real. The Greenland ice cap is melting. Antarctica which has 90 percent of the earth's ice is melting. Mountain glaciers in the Andes and Himalayas and the Siberian permafrost are melting. Deforestation is accelerating. Carbon dioxide and methane gases are rapidly heating up the planet. We are already past 350 parts per million (ppm) of carbon dioxide in the atmosphere – the highest concentration without dangerously heating up the Earth. This means that if this heating up goes unabated, the seas will rise up to six feet and flood coastal cities and cover up islands. In other parts of the world there will be massive desertification, droughts and food collapse. Mega storms will be the norm. There is already a massive die-back of species. There will be social, political and economic crises with mass migration and resource wars. Drinking water will become very scarce and wars will be fought over this life-essential resource. The next ten years will tell the story of our future – misery or happiness.

The opportunity before us is to let go of carbon-based energy, "death-energy" from dead animals and plants, and to invent a sustainable development path for humanity and all life forms. We can and must shift to renewal energy, "life-energy", from the sun, water, wind, geo-thermal, algae and bio-fuels. But we must do this swiftly to avert disaster.

Economic

The global economic crisis we are in the midst of is a result of a financial system that is divorced from nature and social justice. Corporations, treated as persons and driven solely by profit motive, are endangering natural ecosystems and subverting democratic institutions. The opportunity here is to invent a new financial order, to reinvent money, and reinvest value in nature and people. And we must end the madness of the consumption-production cycle and create the Learning Society.

Political

We are in the midst of governance collapse. It is a crisis of democracies which have become plutocracies controlled by banks and insurance companies, the oil and coal industry, other corporations and the super-rich. The opportunity lies in reinventing governance that is participatory, just and in line with sustainable development goals.

Social

The major crises are in healthcare and education. We have an opportunity to catalyze a new commonsense of the universal rights to education and healthcare.

Cultural

We face a crisis of the sunset effect of fear-based fundamentalisms – Christian and Hindu as well as Muslim. Yet through this, the opportunity exists for a shift to an evolutionary Earth story, empathic consciousness and the rise of the Cultural Creatives (Paul Ray).

There is a pathway forward. We need to put an end to our purely production-consumption society, end the unrealistic concept of unlimited growth and drive towards a sustainable, equitable, participatory, just society. We need renewable energy, an equitable financial system, participatory governance, environmental protection, universal healthcare, education for all and gender equality. We need new ways of thinking, new assumptions, and new myths, policies and collective action. Awakenment must proceed and accompany action and commitment. We need to understand how to stay awake and how to act mindfully. We need a "lure of becoming" that draws us out of the present delusion and morass toward a hoped-for future.

Within this very moment of crisis, a **new civilization** is emerging. It is an Earth-based civilization of sustainable human development. In this new civilization, people will increasingly embody a consciousness of being part of the living Earth, of being part of the life force of our beautiful planet. We are all Earthlings. All people and all life forms are our brothers and sisters. We have a common future or no future at all. In the new civilization, people will embody behavior that is empathic and compassionate. People will embody a culture of peace, creativity and learning. People will embody systems, policies and institutions of equality, justice and universal participation in decision-making. And if we do not create such a civilization, the alternative will be chaos, tyranny, suffering and systems collapse.

In the midst of this critical decade we must build a new civilization of sustainable human development country by country, organization by organization, and most importantly, community by community.

The author's first experiences in community development were on the West Side of Chicago working with the Institute of Cultural Affairs, an NGO in the African American ghetto in the 1960s. The NGO was catalyzing a demonstration of how any community in the world could transform itself economically, socially, culturally and politically. The pilot project was named 5th City. As people from outside the community, the NGO's role was to empower, train, equip and connect the local residents to do their own development.

We worked within a geographically delimited area and involved all the people, all age groups and addressed all issues simultaneously which we called integrated human development. We found through hard experience that symbols were the keys to community renewal. 5th City created songs, stories and symbols that inspired local residents to transform their community. There was a sculpture of the Iron Human on 5th Avenue, songs of empowerment in the preschool and in community meetings and stories of heroes doing the impossible and creating a new world. Residents understood that what they were doing was on behalf of the whole world. 5th City was a global human development demonstration project and this was perhaps the most powerful motivation of all.

And we learned that every community has a depth contradiction that is blocking its development that must be addressed. For 5th City it was the victim image – people felt that they were powerless to create their own destiny. One way to counter this was to create empowering songs for the preschool children such as this one: "I am always falling down. But I know what I can do. I can pick myself up and say to myself. I'm the greatest too. It doesn't matter if you're big or small. You live now if you live at all. I am always falling down. But I know what I can do."

Based on the 5th City model we created a participatory planning methodology that any community could use. We took it around the world and launched human development projects in the 24 time zones of the planet. The author helped launch two projects in the Republic of Korea, one on Cheju Island in the village of Kwang Yung Il Ri and one near the DMZ, Kuh Du I Ri. He also worked in village projects in Jamaica (Woburn Lawn) and Venezuela (Cano Negro). Eventually our NGO was working in hundreds of communities around the world including mass replication in India and Kenya.

When the author joined UNDP in 1990, he helped design and launch a global program to renew urban slums and squatter settlements around the world. The LIFE program (the Local Initiative Facility for the Urban Environment) worked in 12 pilot countries around the world in 300 cities. Local residents worked in collaboration with local authorities and NGOs in improving their living environment. We called this "local-local dialogue." Through small grants for micro projects local people improved their solid waste management, potable water, environmental health and education and drainage, gender equality and created local jobs.

At the beginning of this century the nations of the world launched through the UN the Millennium Development Goals (MDGs) initiative. This was the first time in history that the world had agreed on tangible, time bound goals to improve the lives of people all around the world. These goals included eradicating poverty, empowering women, providing early education, protecting the environment and mitigating HIV/AIDS and malaria. Many of us in the UN believed that the key to achieving these goals was in their localization. Therefore, we launched initiatives to localize the MDGs in urban and rural communities around the world, such as Decentralizing the MDGs through Innovative Leadership.

And now, those who care about the future of life on Earth are intending to create a new civilization country by country, community by community, lesson by lesson, story by story. This is our noble cause.

III. 21st Century Public Service and Transformative Leadership for Sustainable Human Development

Public service in the 21st century faces many challenges and opportunities. In the midst of the breaking down of an old civilization and the emergence of a new civilization, public service is now called more than ever before to provide innovative leadership for sustainable human development.

There are many styles of leadership which follow a developmental progression (Dennis Emberling). First leadership can be authoritarian, exploitative and coercive. Here the leader is the boss, dictator or employer. Next leadership can be bureaucratic with the focus on rules and roles; here the leader is a manager, administrator or "parent." The third stage of leadership is pragmatic with a focus on results. Here the leader is a guide. Next, leadership can be based on values and principles. Here the leader is a facilitator, coordinator or coach. And finally, leadership can be systems-based with a concern for multiple perspectives. Here, there are no managers but true delegation of responsibility to all members of the team.

What then are the most effective means in this critical decade with which to build a new civilization country by country, community by community, organization by organization? **Transformative leadership** approaches are an essential key to unlock the potential of countries, communities and organizations. From four decades of international development work the author is aware of many leadership methods and approaches which have been applied within UN programmes, national governments, NGOs, private companies, local communities and universities. A few of the many effective ways of building creative countries, organizations and communities through innovative leadership follow.

Change requires new systems, policies and institutions but these alone are not enough. In order to create effective change, we must also transform individual consciousness and behavior and collective culture. These four dimensions of leadership based on Ken Wilber's quadrants of integral development are all essential: change that is both individual and collective and internal and external.

Four Quadrant Integral Framework		
	Interior	**Exterior**
Individual	- Consciousness - Mindset - Awareness - Values - Attitudes	- Behaviour - Interpersonal - Relational - Partnerships - Group Skills
Collective	- Culture - Myths/Stories - Rituals/Rites - Symbols - Norms	- Environment - Organizations - Institutions - Systems - Policies

The individual/interior dimension of integral leadership includes the consciousness, mindset, awareness, values and attitudes of the leader and his/her development of these in other individuals. The individual/exterior dimension includes the individual behaviour of the leader, interpersonal relations, partnerships and group skills and her/his development of these with other individuals. The collective/interior dimension of leadership includes the leader's work with and transformation of cultural beliefs and values, myths and stories, rituals and rites, symbols and norms for the betterment of society. And the collective/exterior dimension of leadership includes the leader's care and re-creation of the natural and built environment, organizations, institutions, systems and policies.

Within each of these quadrants of leadership we must work on four levels of transformation: physical/sensory, psychological/historic, mythic/symbolic and unitive/spiritual. These four levels as delineated by Dr. Jean Houston in her social artistry work are all essential for effective change to take place.

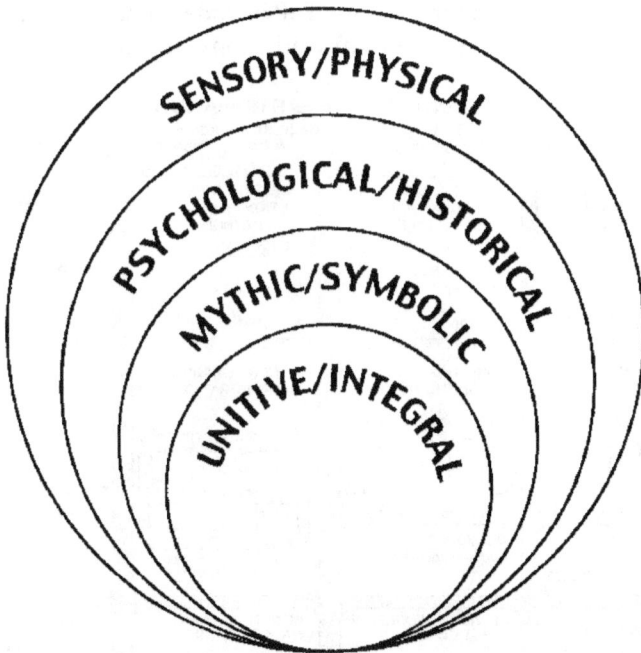

The sensory/physical level of social artistry leadership concerns the enhancement and activation of a leader's senses especially of deep listening and visionary seeing but also of touch, taste and smell so as to be fully present to ones physical existence. This level includes the keen use of all the senses in relation to the natural and built environment, culture and individual and group behaviour. The psychological/historical level of social artistry leadership includes the deepening of individual and collective memory and emotion, personal psychological history, personal story, dream and reflection, both in the leader and those the leader serves. The mythic/symbolic level of social artistry leadership includes the use and powerful interpretation of myths, stories, heroes/heroines and symbols of culture and religion so as to motivate the society to reach its human development goals. The unitive/integral level of social artistry leadership includes the experience and mysterious awareness of the unity and interconnectedness of all of life, sense of oneness with others, self transcendence, spirituality, deep motivation, love and sense of calm and trust.

The third set of methods that is part of innovative leadership is the Technology of Participation or ToP. This array of effective leadership methods was developed by the Institute of Cultural Affairs (ICA) with which the author worked for 21 years. ToP includes, among others, methods of effective group discussion, group workshops and strategic planning.

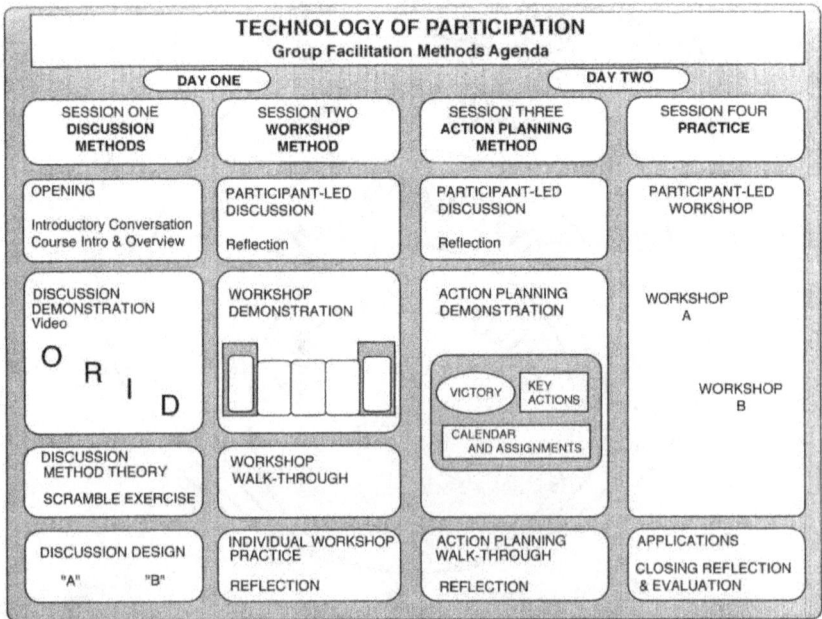

TECHNOLOGY OF PARTICIPATION
Group Facilitation Methods Agenda

DAY ONE		DAY TWO	
SESSION ONE DISCUSSION METHODS	SESSION TWO WORKSHOP METHOD	SESSION THREE ACTION PLANNING METHOD	SESSION FOUR PRACTICE
OPENING Introductory Conversation Course Intro & Overview	PARTICIPANT-LED DISCUSSION Reflection	PARTICIPANT-LED DISCUSSION Reflection	PARTICIPANT-LED WORKSHOP
DISCUSSION DEMONSTRATION Video	WORKSHOP DEMONSTRATION	ACTION PLANNING DEMONSTRATION	WORKSHOP A
O R I D		VICTORY / KEY ACTIONS	WORKSHOP B
		CALENDAR AND ASSIGNMENTS	
DISCUSSION METHOD THEORY SCRAMBLE EXERCISE	WORKSHOP WALK-THROUGH		
DISCUSSION DESIGN "A" "B"	INDIVIDUAL WORKSHOP PRACTICE REFLECTION	ACTION PLANNING WALK-THROUGH REFLECTION	APPLICATIONS CLOSING REFLECTION & EVALUATION

3   ©THE INSTITUTE OF CULTURAL AFFAIRS. 1996

The ORID group conversation method takes people on a four part journey from Observation (what do you notice about the topic?), to Reflection (what are your associations and feelings about this?), to Interpretation (what does this mean to you?), and finally to the Decisional (what relationship do you decide to take to this?) concerning what to do because of the discussion.

The ToP workshop method includes six steps: 1) deciding the rational and experiential objectives, 2) setting the context, 3) brainstorming, 4) grouping of data, 5) naming of clusters of data and 6) reflecting on the group's consensus.

The ToP strategic planning process uses the workshop method for each step and enables a community or organization to 1) articulate the shared vision of their hoped-for future, 2) analyze what could block or enable that vision, 3) create broad strategic directions to achieve the vision, 4) identify tactical systems to achieve the strategies, and 5) decide what discrete actions or implementaries in what timeframe will do the job.

These are only three of many, many innovative leadership approaches that have been effectively applied around the world with governments, NGOs, local communities and corporations. If made further use of in public service, public administration and governance over the coming years, they can have profound results both for the individual leader her/himself and for those with whom she/he works and serves as a leader. If a designated or elected leader makes use of these types of innovative methods, whole organizations, institutions and communities will begin to mirror and emulate the leader's own awareness and prowess creating a powerful multiplying effect throughout the society. Can you imagine the use of any of these leadership approaches in a cabinet meeting or a parliament and what a difference they could make?

IV. Thematic Discussion and Action
Let us look at four thematic areas related to leadership:
1. Leading with integrity and inventiveness in public governance.
2. Engaging citizens and civil society organizations to promote effectiveness, accountability and transparency in reconstruction and recovery strategies after nature disasters.
3. E-leadership capacity development.
4. Leading innovations in gender-responsible service delivery.

With a social philosophy inspired by the Universal Declaration of Human Rights and in light of the challenges and opportunities of this Critical Decade, these themes provide an opportunity to articulate new pathways of transformative leadership and innovative governance. These pathways will in turn help clarify social discourse about future global, national and local scenarios and inspire people around the world to do what is needed at this moment in history to bring into being a new civilization of sustainable human development.

These four themes taken together identify and delineate a new style and practice of leadership and governance that embodies integrity, creativity, participation of all the people in a society, gender equity and use of information and communication technology and social networking. This is what is meant by transformative leadership - leadership that can respond effectively and profoundly to the multitude of challenges facing humanity at this critical moment and facilitate the creation of a new civilization.

Transformative leadership moves a society from a problem-solving mode to a whole systems design mode. It helps transform individual mindsets, values and behaviour, and collective culture and institutions. The transformative leader is deeply concerned and committed to creating the conditions in a society that enable each woman, man and child to realize her/his full potential. Transformative leadership makes use of participatory, interactive methods to ensure that each person's voice and wisdom is heard and felt in social dialogue and policy making.

The transformative leader is a social artist and makes use of myths, stories, rituals, symbols and metaphors to motivate the society to imagine and reach its future vision. Transformative leadership makes use of the very latest information technologies to enable the population to participate in governance processes at every level. The transformative leader is a person of deep personal integrity and empathy who manifests compassion for other people. He/she is committed to being the servant of the people in helping everyone to live well and to die well. Transformative leadership is responsive to present and potential danger and disasters and helps prepare and engage the population in doing what is needed to avert and deal with natural disasters such as climate chaos and human-made suffering such as armed conflict. The transformative leader has a profound belief in universal human rights and is a powerful advocate for the empowerment of women, minorities, elders and youth.

Transformative leadership works to create strong democratic institutions and processes of governance. If transformative leadership were found in legislatures, executive offices, bureaucracies, courts, electoral commissions, NGOs and corporations, what a transformation we would see in the larger society! The transformative leader does everything in her/his power to help make a better life for all the people. In order to do this, he/she manages her/his ego, pride, greed, fear, anger and hatred and practices concern for and understanding toward all people.

How do we each work in our own countries, organizations and communities with renewed vision and practical tools for the betterment of their societies? How do we stay networked electronically and continue to challenge and encourage each other? How can we make use of new methods of leadership and help create new institutions of participatory governance? How can we design new systems and structures, as well as new policies, programmes and projects that will put into practice these insights?

Concluding Questions

What if we are in the midst of a turning point in human history - from despair to hope, from greed to compassion, from impoverishment to empowerment? What if we are indeed the people that the world has been waiting for? What if we are the catalysts and servants that history requires at this time? What if we are able to mobilize people in such a way as to respond to climate chaos, increasing poverty, the HIV/AIDS pandemic, gender-inequality and economic collapse? What if we embody integrity, creativity, effectiveness, accountability and transparency in everything we say and do?

What if we are the transformative leaders who call our fellow and sister citizens to join us in the greatest and noblest of tasks – to Build the Earth - to create a New Civilization - to catalyze Sustainable Human Development? What if these are indeed the times and we are indeed the people?

References:

Houston, Jean. Jump Time: Shaping Your Future in a World of Radical Change. New York: Tarcher/Putnam, 2001

Wilber, Ken. A Brief History of Everything. Melbourne; Hill of Content, 1996

Work, Robertson. "Civil society innovations in governance leadership: International demonstrations of integral development, the technology of participation and social artistry." pp 112-131. Engaging Civil Society. Cheema and Popovski, Ed. Tokyo: UN University Press, 2010

Websites:
Innovative Leadership Services. www.innovativeleader.org
Institute of Cultural Affairs. www.ica-international.org
Integral Institute. www.integralinstitute.org
Jean Houston Foundation. www.jeanhoustonfoundation.org

(This chapter is based on a paper prepared by the author for UNDESA's Global Forum on Transformative Leadership, June 2011, Dar es Salaam, Tanzania)

Sharing Approaches that Work: Personal Change as ICA

Lawrence E Philbrook

I'M THE GREATEST
I'm the greatest. You're the greatest.
That's the way life is.
When you show it.
When you know it.
You are free to live. Hey!!
(5ᵗʰ city pre-school song 1964)

The verse above is a reminder that each of us makes a choice everyday about who "the me is I choose to be." This song was created after hearing Mohammed Ali (a black, American boxer in the early '60's) chanting "I'm the greatest". ICA was working in the inner city catalyzing new opportunity and new life in a decaying urban slum. Its declaration was transformed into this song we sang in the 5ᵗʰ City Chicago Pre-school, ICA's first Human Development Project. I still use this in my work with communities, companies and with individuals because the message is just as shocking and revealing.

YOU ARE THE GREATEST! WHAT CHOICES ARE YOU MAKING WITH THAT GREATNESS?

With the focus on how to be responsible for one's own future, and providing a safe environment in which to make choices to do that, ICA from its beginning raised the question to individuals and communities about their purpose, intention and what living into that purpose and intention might look like. As answers appeared, ICA's supported communities and individuals in their journey.

ICA's purpose: To care for and promote human development.

Core strategies then and now:

- **Awakenment:** Literally waking people and communities up, to be fully present to the Now, aware of being related to a larger universe, helping them to identify and describe their current reality, then through that new perception to see possibility and assume responsibility for oneself and the world.

- **Engagement:**   Discover, create and share useful, creative ways to participate in building the new society, "always in the making."

- **Formation:** Day to day living the life, impacting ongoing communities of location, practicing and caring all of which embody ICA values and strategies

From the early days, personal development was in the context of our purpose to serve and develop communities.

Awakenment

The best way for me to illustrate the impact of ICA on individual change is to tell my own story and stories of others.

The first time I remember choosing to be a part of the purpose of ICA, I was 16, had taken a course called Cultural Studies-1 which described the seven revolutions that were going on at that time. We were asked what relationship were we willing to take to these revolutions. The seven were seen in 1969 as:

1. Women
2. Youth
3. Third World Development
4. Expansion of the multinational corporation
5. Education
6. Minorities
7. Local Community.

One question we were asked in CS-1 was, *"What would be the three points in your speech to the citizens of a village in China on their being world citizens?"* I was sitting in Denton, Texas. The world was in the midst of the cold war and the "they" was communist China and … I then realized the underlying question had only partly to do with China but totally with me and what was I going to do to care for the whole world? When I got home

I called my sister Paula and said "I am ready to go". I asked basically this same question to a group of teachers at Hua-Guang High School, Nanning, China in May, 2012.

When looking at awakenment for ICA the questions in different forms and different times have been:

1. Who Am I? Where Is The World? Where Am I In This World?

2. What Is My Story About Who I Am And Our Stories About Who We Are In This World?

3. What Might The World Become To Make It Viable For All? What do I do?

4. What Is My Responsibility In Moving Toward That?

This is the basic framework. We have worked with this as staff, as families, as communities and also always as individuals. How do we make these questions available to others? Over the years we have developed training and reflective formats to enable these same questions to be asked in diverse cultural contexts.

A necessary doorway to awakenment is vulnerability

Vulnerability has to do with honestly facing and respecting myself, then being totally honest about my community and in allowing myself to see others as they are. This is not about judgment. It is about exposing the images or mental models that "I" am operating out of and that "we" are operating out of. ("Mental models are the deeply ingrained assumptions, generalizations, and images of the world and of the organization itself" as described by Peter Senge in "The Fifth Discipline"). Vulnerability is about sharing more of my internal conversations. It is about sharing my answers, but more importantly my questions.

Vulnerability is experiencing risk and deciding in the midst of that experience to expose myself for the sake of my own and the community's learning.

Vulnerability includes sharing my own experiences in such a way that I feel the risk myself. From this sense of risk emerges a sense of respect when in the midst of some fear and uncertainty, I can decide to deepen the dialogue.

At any moment of personal vulnerability a doorway opens, a choice to go deeper into understanding what is going on or a choice not to is made. Sometimes the other person is not ready or able to handle the vulnerability they experience in another person; sometimes they are. When I experience an act of vulnerability in another, I may not appreciate it. I may even reject it. This is part of the risk involved in being vulnerable.

Respect includes honoring the expression of another, while also honoring my own perception of what is going on. I can honor you for being a human being without automatically agreeing with everything you say.

In choosing to move this way, *how do we sustain the journey of the group while maintaining a level of safety that encourages exploration of vulnerability for individuals and the group?* There is no set pattern for this, but there are some hints from experiences of other groups.

Building safety involves developing disciplines of practice:

1) **Listening**: As an individual I can hear only by listening. This is not just about words but listening totally to the other and to myself. This involves suspending my own thoughts and opinions for the moment so I can hear. I find silence is a helpful practice in opening myself up to really hearing. In a group, a few moments of silence can facilitate much deeper listening and sharing.

2) **Paying attention**: An important skill in deepening understanding is to pay attention to what is happening as deeply as you can, rather than what I think should be happening. Individual and group meditation helps develop these skills. How safe does to group feel to itself and to its members? What is really happening? What is causing me to feel vulnerable? Where is the group feeling vulnerable?

3) **Speaking**: The window for me to others is through my speaking. Speak appropriately what you feel needs to be said rather than worrying about whether it is right, whether it's enough or too much. Speak your stories and your pictures of life. Sharing your mental models and assumptions may seem risky, but it facilitates the deepest learning and sharing.

4) **"Action removes the doubt that theory cannot solve."** Begin to open the doors now; there is a greater risk by keeping them closed. Start softly because what you experience as your own vulnerability may unintentionally expose the vulnerability of another before they are fully prepared for it.

Choose your life. About fifteen years ago my mother wrote me a letter to say she had chosen to be happy, so she was going to change her language to reflect that she is choosing her own life rather than having it chosen for her. She ended the letter by saying "I am going to stop writing now because I choose to go to dinner." This in place of "I have to run."

Life is about choices; it is about looking at this group, looking at myself as this individual and choosing to risk.

Engagement

Now that I am awake comes the new question of meaningful engagement; what does authentic involvement look like?

When I first began working in communities I did not really pay attention to the individuals involved but only the organizations or communities. I noticed people as people, but was not really aware that each individual is also transforming at his/her own rate of speed and depth, even while the community is changing. Engagement is about how individuals discover, create and share useful ways to participate in building the future that is always in the making.

Facilitation as a pathway to engagement

When I arrived in India in 1977, I got off the train in Parbhani to assist a local team in doing comprehensive community development. I was 23 and ready to go. I was committed, but completely unclear about what I could do to be of help. I was lucky in that sense because I knew that I did not have a clue. My Indian colleagues helped me discover how to use what I did know, what we now call facilitation, and let go of pretending to know the rest. I spent the next ten years focused on creating more and more understanding about how to facilitate. Then I had another awakening and realized we were moving toward using facilitation as a pathway to personal discipline and authentic community.

M. Scott Peck talked about a "real community." As a group we could transcend differences, communicate openly and learn to work together toward a common goal. In our work on engagement we developed tools that supported individuals being heard and committing to action, first with the focus primarily on the "we" and only later with more awareness on the individual and the group.

From a group perspective ICA's ToP methods flowed out from our early community work and were adapted to help a community form, reflect and decide. From a personal side this develops through dialogue, the ability of an individual to articulate and listen to others while tapping into wisdom inside and outside oneself. One of the critical elements of ICA development is exposure to and learning with others. Every group with which we work provides an opportunity to grow.

My basic image of a facilitator: This quote has been very helpful in describing spirit-based facilitation as an interaction in which both the facilitator and the group or individual are together discovering the new…

"Being a Midwife"

Two critical images "The wise leader does not intervene unnecessarily" and "Facilitate what is happening rather than what you think ought to be happening."

From the Tao of Leadership by John Heider

Guidelines for engagement:

* Providing what another needs but cannot at the moment provide for him/herself. This is a test for facilitating what another needs from me, no more no less.

* Connecting with the other's "deeper self" and letting that deeper self direct the facilitation, coaching, mentoring, healing. This may sound metaphysical, but it is simply focusing an intention which enables one to care for another without imposing or trying to control.

* Higher purpose context and expanded perspective as necessary for long lasting contribution. Higher purpose context is also by intent, but it's helpful to know my unconscious is always working for me, taking in information and reweaving my context in ways my conscious mind may not have yet perceived (From David Brooks, "The Social Animal."

Formation

Day to day living, ongoing communities of practice and care which embody ICA's values and strategies.

All three strategies Awakenment, Engagement and Formation are about one thing: living a disciplined life of choice. In the midst of life's reality what life do I choose? At the level of formation it is about every day behavior and this has to do with the images that have formed in the time of awakenment and engagement to become life patterns.

One of my colleagues in Taiwan, Gail West expressed it this way, *"Imaginal learning is what ICA has always been about – enabling the shifting of one's images or internal pictures of what is, is what directs my beliefs and behavior. As a facilitator or trainer or any person supporting another's development, my understanding is that learning requires image shift. In order for that to happen, a person needs to change the messages that one pays attention to. No change in learning, no change in behavior.*

As a trainer, when I don't intend to raise awareness and shift images, those I work with respond like robots – through memory, rather than what is integrated into behavior."

From the assumption that images determine behavior and that behavior changes only if images are changed (Boulding), came ICA's whole understanding of Imaginal Education. The major image shift we lived was that we could make a difference and that taking action based on an understanding of what needed to happen in the world was what it meant to be a human being. I remember being asked once in a course to list the 5 major problems of the world, after which the next question was, "What are you doing about any of these?" Powerful image change. Many others, e.g. the Bonhoeffer's image of Freedom and Obedience held in tension to enable Responsibility.... One of the key images was that by making and living our choices about the future, we are living out on the white-hot point of historical change and it is possible we will be alone.

I always thought of myself as a group facilitator and that the personal work on dialogue and spirit I was doing was personal, not facilitation. I remember my shock when the CEO of a company I was working with said, "I need to pay you for the coaching you have been doing for me." I responded, I am not a coach, I'm a facilitator. He said "Coaching is the art of facilitating the performance, learning and development of another. It is a joint process to help individuals with personal and/or professional needs, in the development of their full potential and know-how. This is what you have been doing for me, here is your check." I was shocked since I thought of myself as a facilitator charged with group process, not a coach or mentor focusing on an individual. Then I realized I had been a coach and have myself been coached or mentored my whole life.

About this same time, I was involved in a series of community building workshops led by the Foundation for Community Encouragement, which based its work on M. Scott Peck's Community Building process. One of the things we learned was that in any community there are the dynamics of I, You and We. It is important to honor all three. Recognizing this helped me shift my focus as needed to know, do, be what the person or the group needed from me at that moment.

I began to realize our formation strategies which were both corporate and personal. Corporate, in our looking at the organization or community as a living system and personal in equipping individuals with the reflective tools. Always our task is to reveal the choices they are making and the impact of those choices on themselves and others.

We have developed many tools that help individuals. I call them **Facilitator Mentoring Tools.**

Life charting: Appreciation, love for self, understanding of one's own unique and unrepeatable journey. Charting one's life helps bring emotion to the fore to be affirmed and objectified, enables a client to assign meaning to the different parts of his/her life already lived.

Current Standing Point: Everything about oneself in clear objective terms are the more specifics and the better way we go ahead. It is here that creating one's longer term vision begins… What in my life do I want to change?

Vision - prioritized: What I want to have in my life at a particular point in my future stated in terms of what it would look like when it is realized… Again, the more specific, the better; then the decision about which are the most important to my future, and among those which is the fundamental vision without which the others are allowed to go by. A vision does not have to seem possible, only desirable… Working only with what seems possible at this moment is seriously limiting.

Contradictions: What has to change to enable my vision to unfold… From blocks, issues and problems (to the vision), contradictions indicate what is keeping me and what might keep me in the future from having what I want in my life. It's helpful to work here until the client begins to see possibility of making the changes needed.

• Strategic Actions: Making it happen, clearing away the blocks to ongoing success, way beyond working harder to new, bold, strategic activities and projects. What strategies and actions will allow clearing away, overcoming, dealing with the contradictions in such a way that my desired future becomes reality.

- Implementation: Where to focus efforts, review and recreate as needed; where to begin, what to do, creating time-bound objectives and action steps. Necessary revision from time to time by redirecting, possibly moving ahead to new objectives.

- Join with like-minded colleagues who show up on the journey.

- The image of every seriously committed person needing an Impossible Task (from Tracy Goss, The Last Word On Power) is helpful here. An impossible task is just that, therefore, it always fails!... How to understand this is through the ultimate description of an Impossible Task for an individual which is, "Who I am is the future of ....!" Another way of understanding this is, "When I have an Impossible Task, everything I do furthers the possibility of that task!" And others who also have their impossible tasks, find that sometimes we have common cause. *(It's been helpful and releasing to understand that I don't need to necessarily like all of these like-minded people in order to work well with them and that diversity is necessary to maintain a larger perspective.)*

What choice are you making with the next step you take? Whatever the choice, the next step is also a choice...

One of our colleagues was trying to describe ICA. He said "ICA is like sticky rice, once you get it on your fingers it is hard to get it off. ICA is more in love with us than we are with ourselves." My thought when he said this was first embarrassment then a realization that this is the best illustration that finally it is who you choose to Be that is the address on people.

Planning for
Human Development

Bill Staples

Participatory strategic planning (PSP) empowers every person who participates in it and harnesses the latent potential that exists in every person in a group. Because it makes use of natural thinking processes, it does so in a way that seems and feels effortless. ToP® PSP clears away extraneous ideas and agendas that cloud group planning; then it focuses everyone in the group on commitment to the transformation needed to move everyone ahead. The understanding of the contradiction between what exists now and what we want to exist in the future, and of the inherent tension that exists between them, is at the very core of this transformation and is key in human development.

Funders, political leaders and planners often believe that the visible outcome of a plan after it has been implemented is the most important part of the whole exercise, and it is true that ToP® participatory strategic planning has a good track record for getting results.

Consultants and facilitators often believe that the communal nature of people planning together is the most important part, and true enough, a team that plans a community garden together today, can also plan a small business later.

For the practitioner interested in human development a fundamental aspect of participatory strategic planning, however, is the growth and positive change that is occasioned in the practitioner and in the participant. This is the realm of profound human development. Individuals gain courage, a positive outlook and skill that stays with them long after the planning and this drives a transformation toward new leadership.

I still remember the impact I felt at 16 when I was in ICA participatory planning called a "problemat" at the time. The comprehensive questions "What is history calling for?" "What breakthrough does the world need now?" and "What are you committed to?" were far more compelling and from a fresher direction than the individualistic "What goal do you want to achieve?" Being asked to ponder what the world needs rather than what I want was enough to set me on a new course for life. Joaquina Rodriguez

Ruz in Guatemala said it well, *"I am still doing ToP because I see the life transformations in people, just like me when I encountered it for the first time in Santiago when I was 20. I used it first as a volunteer for a long time with no thought of financial benefit, but now I can use it even for my own sustainability."*

Vision

Consider one of the basic first questions of participatory strategic planning in the field of community development.

What do you want to see in place in your community in five years?

There is no doubt that if enough people answer this question and that if enough of those people consider all the answers and look for patterns in those answers that a comprehensive and motivating vision will emerge. ICA and ToP practitioners have asked this question in consensus workshops tens of thousands of times in thousands of communities and the results are always valuable. Communities have created inspiring visions of social self-reliance with better health, education and welfare for families, economic sustainability with small industry, farming and commercial enterprises, and a culturally cohesive identify with better housing, cultural celebrations and caring leadership. Our archive in Toronto and in other ICAs around the world has hundreds of documents of inspiring and compelling long range practical visions that eventually became real, with community songs, symbols and slogans that announced the outcomes of the vision years in advance.

Now consider the planning from the point of view of an individual, like me, who is participating in this visioning and in the development of that individual. Most of us live without thinking too much about the future, caught in our day to day cares and activities, certainly spending little time thinking about our impact on our community and the world. Someone asks me *"What do you want to see in place in your community in five years?"* and really seems to mean it and listens carefully to what I have to say. I find myself realizing that I do want a better world and I do have opinions about the future. Can it be possible that someone really cares what I think? Then I hear many other people repeating some of the same points that I have in my vision, and I see a written Vision Chart emerge that represents what I actually said, and more than that, what everyone said. For a few minutes I see a picture of a different, better world before me, one that I have unconsciously longed for perhaps all my life and that my children actually deserve to live in. This is worth more of my consideration.

This is the initial developmental shift that occurs in an individual who participates in the visioning part of participatory strategic planning. The shift is from the "me" to the "we", from an unconscious to a conscious recognition of an actual community, and from a short term day-to-day preoccupation to a future orientation.

Contradiction

Another basic question in participatory strategic planning, generally asked second, is *"What is blocking us from moving ahead into our desired vision of the future?"* ICA calls an underlying or a root systemic block a contradiction. The 19th century philosopher Hegel described contradiction as the movement between thesis and antithesis out of which emerges synthesis. Contradiction is a tension between what exists now and what will exist in the future, a shadow on the wall of the shape of things to come... we see the outline but the light of reality obscures it. The contradiction is the current pattern of how we live now that says NO to our practical vision—contradicting and negating it. It might be an addictive behaviour that stops us from attaining what we really want to be.

When a community creates a list of all the issues and blocks that hold them back and then analyzes the pattern in those lists, they discover what is really blocking them. There is a collective sigh of relief when the "elephant in the room" has been named and they can finally move ahead. The contradiction can be different in every community but it is a breakthrough when it is finally recognized and named. One city council had a wonderful long range vision but realized that their vision would remain only a dream unless they dealt with their biggest contradiction, council infighting and local petty politics that stalled every effort. One neighbourhood group in Toronto recognized that what they were proudest of, their cultural diversity, was also their biggest block because three ethnic groups did not work together. ICA and ToP® planning practitioners are well-known and trusted for being able to take a group of people on such a journey of discovery. Many communities do not like to have the truth uncovered, but when it is they recognize how important it is to deal with it, and are ready to create strategy together.

How does a contradictional analysis affect an individual? I have found that it can be a moment of real breakthrough and an occasion of great personal growth. For example, when I am enthusiastic in the planning session about a community vision and then stop to consider why it has not already been worked on, I first blame others for not doing their part. The folks "on the other side of the railroad track" never get involved in community events and stay to themselves all the time. It must be the way they were brought up. I do take note, however, that they are here in the planning and have actually agreed that they want the same thing as me. But I don't know them very well and don't know if I should trust them. After all, a couple of them are very big, don't smile much, and have never come out for anything else. But, hold on, that was an interesting comment one of them just made. She said that she's always wanted to help but always felt like an outsider because she has only been here for 15 years. Maybe we should give them a chance to show what they can do. Maybe I judged them too soon. Have I done that to anyone else?

These are the developmental shifts that occur in an individual during a contradiction session. There is a recognition that hanging on to unhelpful patterns of past behaviour gets in the way of what we want. There is an acknowledgement that we all operate from those old patterns, need to change them, and can change them. There is an affirmation that other people have potential that has been ignored or written off. These developmental shifts can be transformative, and the memory of them can remain and encourage all future change.

Strategy

Another basic question in participatory strategic planning, usually the third, is *"What can we do to deal with the blocks and move toward the vision?"*

Strategy shows the way forward by focusing on the logjam of energy that is caused by a contradiction and creates the way forward by releasing that blocked energy. Strategy emerges out of the intention to create a desired future from an existing reality. Those in participatory planning often spark each other's commitment to the plans by balancing ideas that are bold and innovative with ideas that are proven workable and make good sense. The village of Maliwada used stones fallen from centuries of deteriorating buildings to create its new community centre and transformed past despair into new hope. Neighbourhoods in Toronto proposed community street festivals to get citizens to meet each other, to take back the streets from petty gangs, and changed fear into resolve. Many communities support entrepreneurial women's small businesses in order to generate jobs and create new images and options of community leadership.

Strategy sessions in participatory planning are key to the development of an individual because strategies create the realistic but new ways that a person can see him or herself actually engaging and trying to do something new. The way that I experience this in a strategy session is by listening to idea after idea I suddenly hear one strategy that I am convinced will actually work and that I really want to work on. When I see everyone else in the room responding in similar ways to various strategies I now know that we have a brand new situation on our hands. I see many people signing up for the strategies, five or six teams emerge and I become energized and committed to see things through. This is definitely worth my Wednesday and Saturday nights, and I get to meet and learn from new people as well!

The developmental shift that occurs during the strategy session encompasses the decision to try out new things and to take risks that have not been taken before. It also moves one to meet new people and reprioritize one's time and energy. The human development that occurs during a strategy session is not small, and is a direct consequence of having participated in the vision and the contradiction session.

Implementation

The developmental shifts that occur to individuals during the implementation after participatory strategic planning can be even more dramatic. We all know that small success early on turns into bigger success later on. The team activity of building a small village latrine has many of the same elements as building a large health centre at a later date. The food, song and appreciation for colleagues after putting up 500 posters is the same as the food, song and appreciation when the ribbon is cut for the new firehall. The private conversation with the old man down the street who says he will take a positive stand toward the community garden, is as memorable as the conversation with the MP who promises funding for the new water system.

All of us who lead participatory strategic planning at the community level are familiar with the young fellow, or woman, who sits at the back and says little. He is not dressed very well and is a little unsure of himself. We recall he came to several meetings, took some notes, and eventually made some comments in the small team dialogues. We remember his nervousness the first time that a small team assigned him to go up to the front of the plenary and read a one paragraph report out loud. We certainly will never forget it when we saw his name as a co-leader of the communication task force. We were stunned when we heard he made a pitch to the local Rotary and got some core funding for the whole project. Our stun turned to delight when he agreed to represent the project at a regional conference. Our delight became amazement when he came back with letters of interest from five more organizations.

We have seen this person over and over in our experiences with human development. During my three years in the Nava Gram Prayas or New Village Movement in Maharashtra I was a twenty-five year youth helping to organize the work of several hundred ICA staff interns, almost all of whom were village youth from 16-25 years. We dug wells, triple-cropped, set up clinics and preschools, built sewage and electrification systems, planned roads and infrastructure, had lots of community meetings and celebrations, and did it all with very little money. ICA India no longer has those several hundred staff, but all of those people took their experiences and are now leaders in their own communities, or working with government or civil society and making a difference wherever they live. That is the wonder of human development.

I recently heard a presentation about Il N'gwesi, a Masaii village in Kenya in which forty young Masaii village volunteers completed HIV AIDS testing of over 95% of the community population. The whole project had been accomplished using ICA participatory planning. 95% tested was astounding since public health officials often get less than 10% tested. A health researcher from the University of Toronto did a complete study of the project, and the current infection rate was reported as less than 5%, a very small number. The project is supporting those people who have contracted the disease. Detailed health statistics and numbers were compiled and people at the presentation asked questions about the scope of the project, the efficacy of the results, and wondered about the expansion of a health outcome that took over two years. The whole model was quite unique, but seemed expensive and cumbersome to replicate. At the end of the question period a last question was asked, "Whatever happened to the forty volunteers?" The Il N'gwesi speaker said that many of the volunteers got jobs doing similar work in other nearby government jurisdictions! We had become so focused on the health outcomes that we forgot all about the larger human development that had occurred, namely the change in the lives of the volunteers.

I will remember that young man at the planning meeting, those hundreds of Nava Gram Prayas interns, and the forty Il N'gwesi volunteers. At one time or another we all were that young man or woman, those young men and woman. In our own human development within ICA we did not begin our journey as high-functioning facilitators, consultants or practitioners. We began as individuals nervously sitting in a participatory strategic planning meeting wondering if the person up front was really listening.

Participative Leaders Training Program - A Very Special Life Experience

Ana Mari Urrutia Arestizabal

The Beginning

As I was working as the Director in the Child Rehabilitation Center Institute (Instituto de Rehabilitación Infantil), at Santiago, Chile, I became aware of the loneliness, the segregation, and the isolation that our former patients were living in, after they left the Institute as they became older, thus surpassing the age we were supposed to work with them. Then I remembered the Methods of the Institute of Cultural Affairs (ICA), called Technology of Participation (ToP). I sent a project to the Pro Help of Disabled Children Society (Sociedad Pro Ayuda del Niño Lisiado), and it was fully approved by the General Manager Mr. Sergio Oyanedel. We started with enormous optimism to work and practice with it. We included 25 disabled young men and women and 8 University boys with no disabilities. We chose the group very carefully, looking for physically challenged youngsters who had kept their mental capacities and who had studied at the university.

We developed the first program in 2001 and it was quite a test to all the facilitators who worked with us to the best of their ability in order to make this project something really special and unique. Eduard Christensen, Nigel Blackburn, Andrés Christensen, Isabel Rodríguez and others interested in our Methods, worked as our facilitators. The course was called Participative Leaders Training Program (PELP in Spanish). After this first time, we found that using ICA Methods, these youngsters progressed enormously on self management. They discovered that working in teams could help them to develop their own projects. It stimulated their creativity and their possibilities to innovate. And very importantly, they found out that working with others made them forget their isolation and loneliness. Besides, it reinforced their personality, they dared to speak in public, their self image in the general society had changed positively and they acquired a surprising self confidence. We saw that this program could support their inclusion in society and their search to level the opportunities they had as physically challenged youngsters and thus acquired their insertion as members of the working society. As we offered them these leadership tools they were able to design and lead their own projects, think strategically and plan their future accordingly. They definitely achieved the tools to change and innovate their projects and life plans, waking up their inner mentor.

As I think about all those years I worked in Rehabilitation (medically oriented), I realized the enormous effort we did to enable those youngsters to walk, move their limbs and trunk. So they could go to school and even some to the University, however, we had disregarded their vocational orientation and their work possibilities. We hadn't taught them how to think of their future. Surprisingly with these tools we handled them, we had managed to magically give rehabilitation a whole new dimension that was nearer to their real inclusion in the body of society.

The Process Itself

We kept working with PELP Programs each year at the Child Rehabilitation Center Institute in Santiago, and we expanded our work to other Institutes at Antofagasta, Valparaiso, Concepción, and Puerto Montt. Thus, until the year 2010 we were able to develop 18 Programs with the participation of 543 youngsters, both disabled and not disabled. We worked with them on Saturdays, because these participants who were 18 to 35 years old were either studying or working, so our meetings didn't interfere with their normal activities.

PELP has the following General and Specific goals:

<u>General Goal:</u> contribute to enable the presence of physically challenged people in the community and integrate them to society as youngsters with different capacities.

Specific Goals:

a) Promote participants' personal development through programming their activities. This improves their self esteem and changes their attitudes and behaviour positively.

b) Promote participants' training and capacities as group facilitators are using properly the Technology of Participation and practicing it.

c) Support participants' physical and psychological rehabilitation in order to reinforce their social and work.

d) Support participants in improving their management capacities, such as planning, resource generation and participative leadership.

e) Support in participants abilities (successful communication, strategic thinking, individual and group dynamics, team work, organization and project management) that are very helpful in any work.

Methods used in the PELP Process

PELP process starts with the participants' learning the methods and practice of Group Facilitation, according to the Technology of Participation (basic Methods). Besides this, we have exposure visits and finally they develop a project that enables them to practice what they have learned during the year. They practice the Methods working with their teams.

Furthermore, we have different specialists who talk to them about project funding, self esteem, group dynamics and we also include their parents in our Program.

Description of the Basic Methods in Technology of Participation

Basic Methods provide the following benefits:

- They shorten the time spent on solving problems and prevent conflict too.
- They enable groups to discover their real motivations.
- They create a deeper personal commitment.
- They show visible results.
- They save time and money through stimulating group productivity.

Guided Dialogues

It is a structured process that helps planning and eases the exchange of important ideas in a group. It is a way to help participants to commit and be a part of the discussion of difficult subjects. This process is very efficient to lead (facilitate) all types of group communications.

- It promotes leading in meetings and discussions with a clear purpose.
- It quickly captures the best of the insights of the group.
- It allows new ideas and solutions to flourish.
- It allows to ask questions that stimulate discussions and sincere and deep feed-back.

Consensus Workshop

This is a process that implies the active solution of problems, building participation and team work. It channels productively whatever diversity of ideas there may be in a group and enables it to reach decisions that will affect them personally through a consensus they can support. It helps the group to attain new levels of creativity and collaboration.

- It stimulates rational and intuitive thinking.
- It integrates a diversity of ideas.
- It allows the group to reach practical and creative solutions.
- It develops group consensus.

Action Plan

It is a powerful process that helps planning and implementation. It allows a group to quickly arrive to an efficient plan, to organize the resources necessary to develop it and to stimulate individual energy into action.

- You can visualize a successful result.
- It analyses actual realities.
- It creates a practical and realistic plan.
- It maximizes individual commitment.

These methods were created by ICA (Institute of Cultural Affairs), motivated by the need to better activities at rural areas and improving the lives of vulnerable people, all around the globe. Most of the methods were designed between 1947 and the 70's. Its goal is to empower people so they can be the masters of their own destiny and thus be included into the rest of society. All continents have had the chance to use these methods, such as Asia, the West Indies, Australia, Europe, Africa, and North and South America. Maybe the most remarkable characteristic of the Method is that it is simple and that it can be learned only by experiencing it and feeling its results. It only requires interest in it and some supporting materials.

Results and Participants' Opinions

In January 2012 we organized a meeting of various PELPs participants, so as to listen to their inputs on their relevant memories and values of the Program. We could confirm our appreciations on the results of this Program through their own testimonies and through follow-up reports we had done throughout the years.

We have discovered and we keep on doing so after 18 PELPs, how the Technology of Participation helps physically challenged people to develop their personality, their self esteem and it helps them to dare develop new and challenging projects. *Giannina Carvajal (PELP participant and former patient at the Institute) declares "...I think that another very important value of PELP is that it encourages self esteem. There are people with a very low self esteem. These Programs and the opportunity to listen to different life stories encourage our own self esteem...".* **Verónica** **Zambrano** *(PELP participant and former patient at the Institute) also declares"... in my opinion the greatest help we received was that we really learned to trust our own abilities. Sometimes one realizes that one is able to do things and all of a sudden you are convinced that it is so. PELP helped me so much in that area, besides learning how to work in teams, and to decide what to do. I give in a little and you give in a little, and we learn to accept that your idea is better than mine...".*

In our country, physically challenged people are given less opportunity for participation. They are isolated, abandoned and many times they are overprotected by their families, especially when they are young. We have been able to observe how they change: they feel re-enchanted, empowered, they feel self valued and they can manage themselves. *Ariel (PELP participant and former patient at the Institute) "...the most important thing to me was to be able to socialize with all of you, who are my peers. Even though I had assisted to the Institute as a child I had never socialized with my peers in other kind of activities as I did with PELP. I liked that very much. As a teenager, to know the problems we are having at this stage of our lives, besides all the problems we already have, I felt enriched through their experiences. That was relevant to me".* As a result we could perceive in these youngsters a need to be the leaders of their own lives, the need to promote and participate in a variety of new projects. We could observe in them, great changes as individuals and as members of the general society. **Maylin Saravia** *(PELP participant and former patient at the Institute) "...I was nervous and fearful during those first days. I was afraid of the new challenges I was going to experience. Nevertheless it was an enriching experience not only for me but for all the kids in my group. I developed my personality and independence and made very good friends. Eleven years ago I was studying at the Institute and had other friends and illnesses. This was an enriching experience that helped us to be leaders and to be independent..."* All this experience makes them feel their self value: to be able to act, to speak in public. They start trusting their own abilities, recognizing their weaknesses and they work hard in order to overcome them. This means a great effort to attain the inclusion of these youngsters into society and into their communities. **Alvaro Díaz** *(PELP participant and former patient at the Institute) "...the value of participation and of team work is very important. We saw very shy people overcome their shyness and we were very tolerant with each other."* They are capable to express themselves and to make others listen to their insights and at the same time they start respecting different opinions. They learn to be tolerant and to debate empathic and assertively, accepting a diversity of opinions and expressing their own thoughts without disqualifying their peers. Besides, they acquire a better disposition to take responsibility and to commit to their work. **Oscar Alvarez** *(PELP participant and former patient at the Institute) "...team work was the most important part, and being respectful to others. I participated on PELP 2, it was very important to respect other's ideas and respect our own convictions...".*

There is an environment of fellowship because of this feeling of self value and tolerance. They share their ideas with respect, enthusiasm and joy. Links of real affection are created amongst them that last through time. **Patricio Suárez** *(PELP participant with no disability) "....I believe that my fellow participants and their perseverance to be there each Saturday is what keep us together as real companions, besides the joy that we felt at each meeting..."*

All these values put together, establish some sort of special magic so as to change the spirit of PELP participants to a more realistic life project for their future. We think that the possibility of talking amongst peers of all those different issues that worry them opens the possibility to deeply define and clarify their anxieties.

Learning ICA Methods gives them the opportunity to use a new work tool, that does not consider whatever activities they are into and they let them strengthen their abilities; it allows them to adapt the tools to different contexts, feeling secure about their choices because they are new, didactic and dynamic. This helps their creative efforts and helps them to change. The facilitator supports and leads these processes without involving himself in them, always trying to keep close contact, warmly and affectionately in order to lighten up the thoughts of all participants.

As a consequence of all this "magic", combined with learning the Methods we could appreciate that they were stimulated to participate and thus create different organized projects in and out of the Program as they became active participants in their near future. They were able to take the necessary actions in order to attain human and economic resources. This allows them to practice the exercise of self management and team work.

Team work is the foundational rock of these Methods and it personally involves all participants. We believe that these Methods are fundamental tools for the inclusion of vulnerable people into their communities. *Isabel Rojas (PELP participant and former patient at the Institute) "... this participation process is really natural: they teach you Methods but it really is a spontaneous process that happens in each one of us and it has infinite possibilities and adaptations. You can use it at work, with your boss, your friends, at home. It's a natural process that can be used in all places and I think that's the reason why we created such deep affective links. It orders your mind and you can use it when you get up in the morning until you go to bed at night, and that's relevant..."*

The physically challenged youngsters' families have a considerable influence in their children's participation and we deeply value the opinions of their fathers and mothers who through these Methods are able to liberate their children and lead them into being independent. Their age (18 to 30 years) is the time in their life development when they are supposed to take big decisions that will influence strongly their life projects and it is precisely at this point where the disabled individual has to attain his or her independence, concentrate on their future education and/or work, they have to decide to have their own families and in their definite inclusion in the general society. *Cristian Olivares' Mother declares.... "I remember their companionship, team work, and the lack of discrimination amongst us. These are values that last for a life time. In my case I saw that my son shared the same thing that you were talking about. He had always felt different, not equal to other boys. He used to say... "not me, I can't, I'm disabled". Here at the PELP he finally understood that he was just one more and that he had the same opportunities, his own opinions and the right to speak up and talk about his feelings. In the family (I have two physically challenged children) they were usually treated as the "special" little boys that were kept aside from all activities. On birthday parties, all the children ran to the piñata and there they stayed sitting by themselves, eating the little birthday cake while all the others were taking active part in the party. My son learned here that it was not like that: that he didn't have to stay away from the group, that he was a part of the family too as he was a part of society. After these courses you could see him at school lecturing his school mates. That was a great pride!!..."*

Through this training in the Program for Participative Leaders, they have been able to create new organizations and insert themselves little by little in the work they create and manage themselves. We have two groups: one of them is called NEW LEADERS PRO INNOVATION and THE ENTREPRENEURS in Santiago and a second one at Valparaíso called ENTREPRENEURS IN ACTION. They have been able to attain projects through entities of the Chilean Government and some international organizations. ***Daniella Gorgollón*** *(PELP participant and former patient at the Institute; she is part of the Board at Entrepreneurs in Action) declares... "getting to meet the group, coming over every Saturday was a great incentive: it was like waiting for Saturday so as to go to the PELP, feeling that there were other individuals like me, people that feel as I do. Before we were part of the Entrepreneurs in Action, we were individuals that had their own anxieties, but we didn't have the strength we acquired when we got together as a group. Our PELP was very important in this, it's an opportunity to take advantage of..."*

Other testimonies:

Debora Fuentes *(PELP participant and former patient at the Institute)... "I believe that it is relevant that we are now able to destroy the barriers that exist towards disability, the prejudices. The different people that were in my group were a novelty; it makes the Program new and different even for those who don't know us. We lived in a bubble. Even to us, the fact of going out and show ourselves, not being afraid of what others might say or think, being equal. The natural process of learning is different for each person, everyone as a different way of approaching the information and then act accordingly. PELP is a polisher of rough diamonds that can finally shine with their own inner light. Each of us is a hero and I include myself in this. Each of us could write a book, a wonderful book, a super valuable one..."*

PELP as also collaborated in helping the awareness of the importance of real and realistic inclusion into communities and society in general. Some testimonies make this clear:

Mauricio Díaz *(Occupational Therapist at the Institute)... "about diversity...PELP helps to accept diversity, to make it natural, it's just there. All the issue of normality broadens, we start looking at ourselves and at our society in a different way..."*

Esteban Saavedra *(PELP participant and former patient at the Institute)... "my attention was taken by the fact that we talk about integration, but here at the PELP we were inversely integrated: we brought it from the outside, how do we integrate others in to our world? And that's exactly what we did...."*

Oscar Alvarez *(PELP participant and former patient at the Institute)... "the most important thing was team work and respect towards each and everyone. Respecting the ideas of all others. It was also very important to respect our own convictions...."*

Marta Neira... *"This is an inclusion Program for the physically challenged, a project on personal development...."*

Transforming Organizations: ICA Approaches that Work

Bill Staples

Organizations in the 21st century experience many pressures that drive them to change in regular, irregular and sometimes dramatic ways. Some of these pressures are external emanating from shifts in society that affect the purpose and function of the organization. Pressures also exist within the organization itself from employees and internal stakeholders who grow and change over time based on their own expectations and opportunities. In this paper, both are examined, along with ToP and ICA methodological responses.

Transformational Drivers from External Pressures

a) Mass migrations from rural to urban populations are rapidly shifting the demographics of regional populations and markets. Cities are now home to new immigrant populations each requiring supports and services in their own language with their own ethno-cultural style. In order to accommodate these shifts organizations are changing the products and services they deliver and the way they deliver them. Governments and the private sectors slowly add or change employees to keep up with the segmentation of populations in their clientele. Because ToP is values-based, it has proven to be a ready-made solution for companies working with such diversity and for creating the new organizational values to support it.

b) The intense interest in solving large-scale environmental problems is affecting most organizations. Any programmatic focus beyond 'reduce, reuse, recycle' requires a more sophisticated whole-systems approach, and needs it for all levels within the organization. ToP has a whole systems analysis and approach which actually prepare people to think through and implement the changes and to create feedback loops between the resource, production, and distribution systems within a company.

c) Communities of interest and practice have been common in many professional associations and are now being developed within industries and in very large companies. While social media and other internet sharing is constantly promoted to communities of interest and practice because of its commercial value, community knowledge and wisdom is created as a result of deep reflection and critical thinking spurred by challenging dialogue and conversation. Face-to-face communication and synthesis which spurs knowledge creation is a domain in which ToP excels, generating consensus on new insight from data and information.

d) Global competition drives companies to increase productivity through team problem solving and front-line creativity. Both of these are supported by continuous improvement and staff engagement. Managers are no longer surprised when "bottom-line productivity" drives them to facilitate staff involvement. ToP excels at staff involvement and, in addition, generates trust and commitment. ToP balances the intensity of productivity with the style of respect. Some organizations put their entire staff through ToP training and that leads to a more productive, happier and respectful workplace with longer staff retention.

e) A wired world in which staff have immediate access to as much information as their supervisors have driven a decrease in the levels of hierarchy within organizations. The speed of information flow has increased exponentially. In many cases this has generated matrix or cluster structures in which front line staff from different organizations collaborate without the need for much hierarchical accountability. Just as Linux is a native operating system for the collaborative nature of the internet, ToP is a native operating system for matrix and cluster organizations with participatory values.

ToP practitioners and ICA staff have documented the use of ToP within organizations to respond to all these pressures in many countries. A survey of 120 ToP practitioners in 2009 (Wiegel, 2009, http://www.surveymonkey. com/sr.aspx?sm=eG6ZhS_2fmPemtaNd2svDXrP1_2fSnvksRAVgyyIg_2f1lX2U_3d) showed that while less than 30% facilitate within large private sector organizations, about 60% practice ToP facilitation within private or public sector organizations. Strategic planning was the largest use of ToP, but team retreats, conferences, regular workgroup meetings and problem solving all made use of ToP methods. Extensive ToP documentation can be found for transformations within banks, insurance companies, the financial sector, manufacturing concerns, hospitals and health systems, universities and education systems, federal and state government departments in many countries, regional and municipal governments, and some UN agencies (Burbidge, (1998), *Beyond Prince and Merchant*, Kumarian Press; Spencer, (1986), *Winning Through Participation*, Kendall Hunt; Wilson, Harnish and Wright, (2003) *The Participative Way*, Team Tech Inc.; Troxel, (1993), *Participation Works*, Miles River Press; Williams, (1993), *More than 50 Ways to Build Team Consensus*, Corwin Press; Bergdall, (1994), Methods for Active Participation, University of Oxford Press).

Transformational Drivers from Internal Developmental Stages

Analyzing documentation from hundreds of organizations that have experienced a significant change especially during ToP participatory strategic planning, and reflecting on current literature, ICA staff became aware of patterns in the journey of organizational transformation. The pattern was similar to those found in developmental psychology in individuals. Eloquent contributors to those descriptions of development were Richard Smith, Willis Harman, John Hormann, Peter Senge, Harrison Owen, Ken Wilbur and Brian Hall. What became clear was that major changes within organizations were driven not only by outside societal factors and market forces, but also by internal drives toward increasing creativity and responsibility of the staff and stakeholders of the organization itself. Organizations evolved through phases that matched the developmental phases of individuals precisely because individuals within the organization drove those transformations based on their own needs and desires to grow. Four phases created a Map of the Journey of Organizational Development, @1996 ICA Canada.

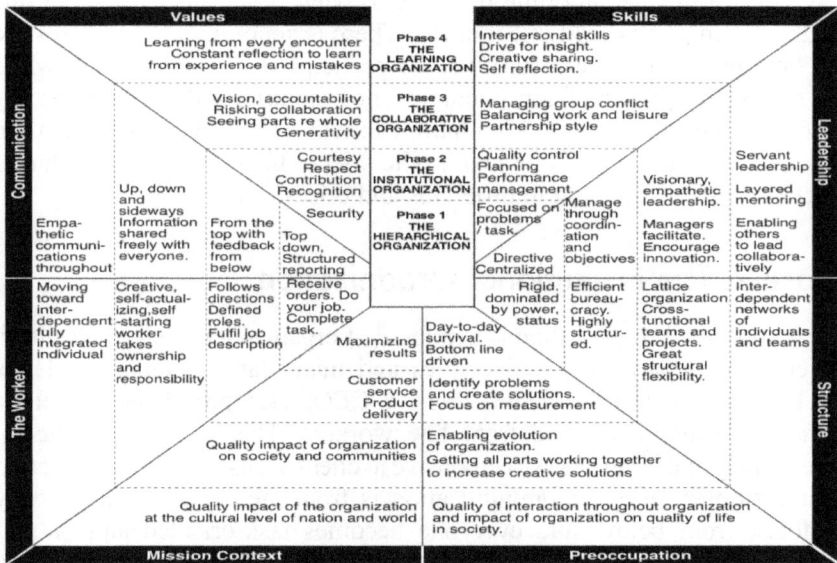

Values

- Phase 4 — THE LEARNING ORGANIZATION: Learning from every encounter. Constant reflection to learn from experience and mistakes.
- Phase 3 — THE COLLABORATIVE ORGANIZATION: Vision, accountability. Risking collaboration. Seeing parts re whole. Generativity.
- Phase 2 — THE INSTITUTIONAL ORGANIZATION: Courtesy. Respect. Contribution. Recognition.
- Phase 1 — THE HIERARCHICAL ORGANIZATION: Security.

Skills

- Phase 4: Interpersonal skills. Drive for insight. Creative sharing. Self reflection.
- Phase 3: Managing group conflict. Balancing work and leisure. Partnership style.
- Phase 2: Quality control. Planning. Performance management. Manage through coordination and objectives.
- Phase 1: Focused on problems / task. Directive. Centralized.

Communication

- Up, down and sideways. Information shared freely with everyone.
- From the top with feedback from below.
- Top down, Structured reporting.

Leadership

- Servant leadership.
- Visionary, empathetic leadership. Layered mentoring.
- Managers facilitate. Encourage innovation.
- Enabling others to lead collaboratively.

The Worker

- Moving toward interdependent fully integrated individual.
- Creative, self-actualizing, self-starting worker takes ownership and responsibility.
- Follows directions. Defined roles. Fulfil job description.
- Receive orders. Do your job. Complete task.
- Maximizing results. Day-to-day survival. Bottom line driven.
- Customer service. Product delivery.

Structure

- Rigid, dominated by power, status.
- Efficient bureaucracy. Highly structured.
- Lattice organization. Cross-functional teams and projects. Great structural flexibility.
- Inter-dependent networks of individuals and teams.

Mission Context

- Quality impact of organization on society and communities.
- Quality impact of the organization at the cultural level of nation and world.

Preoccupation

- Identify problems and create solutions. Focus on measurement.
- Enabling evolution of organization. Getting all parts working together to increase creative solutions.
- Quality of interaction throughout organization and impact of organization on quality of life in society.

Map of the Journey of Organizational Development

©The Canadian Institute of Cultural Affairs, 2005

The following description of the four phases have been abridged from *Edges: New Planetary Patterns, Volume 20, 1998*. Current discussions in some ICA's are underway to describe seven phases, but these four are most readily illustrated and understood.

Phase 1. The Hierarchical Organization

This is a very common type of organization, one in which orders and instructions come directly from the top, like in small family-owned or single shareholder companies, or in police and fire departments. A major strength of the hierarchical organization is the capacity to ride out storms and survive. Another is their clear structure of management and accountability. When difficulties occur the owner or management can operate like a benevolent parent and simply instruct people in what needs to be done to make it over the hump. In such organizations employees are able to get by by doing what they are told and they benefit by the stability they get and by leaving their work at the workplace. A vulnerability can be the failure to use the intellectual capital and creativity of all staff, and of setting priorities by crisis rather than vision. The owner or management may believe in spending time listening to what subordinates say, but this feedback can just as easily be ignored. There is generally a top-down style of communication where staff/worker participation is minimized, while the status and power of top management is maximized. Employees, by following the rules and working hard, can win favour in the organization, and they can become very loyal. The hierarchical organization has a reactive style, responding to problems and crises as they occur.

Phase 2. The Institutional Organization

The institutional organization is a miracle of organization such as hospitals, government departments, universities and many large companies. There are boards of directors, shareholders, a CEO, vice presidents, directors, managers, supervisors, and front line workers. This is a large, efficient bureaucracy and it can be very responsive to client needs with a preoccupation with customer service. Communication is from the top, but informed by feedback from below, and everyone becomes task-oriented and output-focused. The bureaucracy can work well, like a carefully designed clock, with teams, quality controls and management by objectives. People can take on responsibility and creativity and some rise up the ladder of success. Others may stay at the bottom, or may rise to their level of competence...or incompetence. The strength of the institutional organization is great order, predictability, and loyalty to staff and to customers. Responsiveness to clients can be rapid, but responsiveness to social change is glacial. Any attempt to change the organization can bog down in a morass of rules, habit patterns and business as usual. Some people can grow in creativity and responsibility within the silos of departments and branches designed by the institution, but many others just remain in the hierarchy of those silos.

Phase 3. The Collaborative Organization

Interaction is the core characteristic of the collaborative organization. These aim for real teamwork between all members, departments, and stakeholders' groups and are harder to see as actual organizations because they often exist as networks, entrepreneurial groups, consulting firms, professional associations or creative companies. The main difference between collaborative and lower-phase organizations is the free flow of ideas. Management is more concerned about stimulating creativity than preventing unauthorized action. Communication is up, down, and sideways. The missional goal of a collaborative organization is generally to make a quality impact on society. It is concerned about reducing rigidity, and increasing the flow of creativity. The strengths of this situation are obvious: synergy and alignment between the parts of the organization, great structural flexibility, and a mission related to social service. Danger occurs when the organization begins to imagine itself as a big, happy family and staff trust and enjoy one another too much to hold each other accountable to the objective needs of internal and external clients. In a collaborative organization most staff are self-actualizing, and seek to serve society through their work, while the leadership is enthusiastic, visionary and empathetic.

Phase 4. The Learning Organization

The learning organization is blessed with a high degree of interactive learning, an emphasis on human development and a concern with "making a difference." To some extent, this type of organization itself becomes a message to the world, offering its own vision of human relations for the future. Some social media organizations are of this form, in which the medium itself is the message. For learning organizations, outside involvement in the community and personal growth are encouraged as relevant to the organization's vision. Since every encounter is regarded as a learning situation, interpersonal and reflective skills for gaining insight are crucial. Leaders enable others through layered mentoring. A set of core values and operational flexibility enables the organization to deal with rapid change. The great strength of the learning organization is that at its core it honours the needs of the person, the group, and the greater community. The worker is a microcosm of the organization, encouraged to assume responsibility for the whole, beyond his or her job description. The danger of the learning organization is a collapse of structure in favour of "networking" and a calcification of its core values into rules that only a few people understand.

The first two phases are primarily concerned with the patterns of power relations, profit, efficient production and customer service, the preoccupations of the last two phases are with maximizing vision, creativity, interaction, communication and collaboration. The first two phases are about structure while the last two are more about process, though structure remains important.

Different phases of development can exist within one organization. For instance, a primarily hierarchical organization can have a research department that operates in an institutional or even a collaborative mode. A primarily institutional organization can have a training department that operates in a collaborative or learning mode. It is these evolved groups that inspire others to take on more responsibility and evolve as well.

Levels of ToP Impact on Organizational Transformation

ToP methods can be used to proactively envision, plan and implement changes in organizations driven by all the above external and internal factors. ToP is a complete suite of approaches, methods and tools derived from a consistent and unified philosophy based on the unlimited potential of every human being and the ultimate transformative capability of every person.

A rigorous and comprehensive study of the impact of ToP methods within organizations has yet to be done. However, several levels of impact are recognizable from an examination of plans that were generated from ToP facilitation, and the results of implementation. These five levels start from easily observable changes to programs or parts of an organization and end in system wide changes to the organization and the people within it.

1. Enhanced operations

In this simple transformation, specific goals are focused, made more explicit, and a consensus is reached on the operations and structures that will accomplish them. Implementation of this work generally immediately affects a small number of people in some regular way, but it can provide a platform for larger changes. An example of this is a retail outlet that set new sales goals and enhances its staffing, advertising and stocking procedures to accomplish it, or a software firm that decides to provide better training to its employees.

2. New initiatives

In this more complex transformation a previously non-existent entity or initiative is launched and added within an organization. This has both known and unknown effects which may be limited to a small part of the organization, but could spread out to impact others over time. An example of this is a social service agency that decides to start a new research division, or a pharmaceutical company that launches a new product line.

3. Formalized structural change

This can be an important transformation to a large part of an organization, but probably in some regular and rational manner regarding accountability and reporting. It will affect many people in some specific ways. An example is a branch of a bank that is split into two locations, or a health department that takes support staff from all its divisions and consolidates them into one unit.

4. Whole system transformation.

This is a very significant transformation in which external drivers or trends lead an organization to shift its focus, products, services and internal operations, but not necessarily its core mission and principles. It will affect both internal and external stakeholders in unknown ways. Examples of this include a merger of two companies with different operational styles, or the amalgamation of three towns into a city.

5. Values-based, behavioral change

This most profound transformation occurs when the fundamental values and purpose of an organization or department change and necessitate behaviour shifts of every person. It will affect every stakeholder and employee in a very personal way. Examples of this are a non-profit, mission-driven organization mutating into a for-profit, share-holder company, a catholic hospital transitioning to a government-run public health centre, or a charity taking on the role of a regulatory body.

Each of these transformations and levels of impact are supported by the ICA stance of unlimited potential in every human, the ICA theory of imaginal education and its link to behavioural change, the ToP participatory strategic planning process, the ToP consensus workshop and focused conversation methods, historical scan, model building, and many other ToP and ICA processes. These allow the disciplined practitioner to plan the journey of change and imbed the transformation in the structures of the organization with the conscious choice of the participants.

The ToP Practitioner's Dilemma

Most experienced ToP practitioners are able to guide a journey of transformation if they are well-grounded in their own stance, understand the link between image and behaviour, and are disciplined and methodical in the application of ToP processes and tools. ToP practitioners, however, experience a two-fold dilemma. First, the client and his or her organization may be unaware of the depth of transformation needed within the organization. They may refer to the change in terms of "increased productivity and effectiveness" which does not come close to the profound human change which may be needed by the client. Since a productivity paradigm and its language is the only one that the client may be familiar with, the ToP practitioner will be forced to use that language and metaphor to describe the process and outcomes knowing that better language, but more provocative, would be more helpful to describe the fundamental shift that may occur. The second dilemma is that the ToP practitioner will be aware that he or she, too, will be subject to a personal shift and transformation during the process, and may or may not be ready for it. All ToP practitioners know full well that the clients they choose to work with have a personal and long term impact on them. This is not something one generally tell one's client for fear of sounding unprepared.

Facilitating for Geographically Dispersed Organisations

Catalina Quiroz Niño & Luz Marina Aponte Gálvez

T he Institute of Cultural Affairs, Spain ('IACE' initials in Spanish) has used video conferencing with worldwide religious groups to promote a greater participation in strategic and action planning processes; and in the sharing of working practices across continents. ICA's Technology of Participation (ToP) methodologies, such as the Focused Conversation Method, were used to facilitate participation offered by new technologies.

ICA Spain, together with its social enterprise partner, Empower started working with The Oblata Sisters of the Holy Redeemer who work with women in contexts of prostitution in 5 continents. They recognised that the phenomenon of prostitution had become globalised and required new responses. This meant ensuring the participation of Sisters and lay people in policy decision-making, which required a change in their organisational structure to one in which power was shared more horizontally.

ICA Spain worked with them to design and facilitate their new strategy. This was started by a face to face participatory strategic planning session, followed by a series of virtual meetings using video conferencing technology. Virtual working teams were created spanning a variety of countries. Facilitative leadership processes were used to create a new global identity and enhance relationships between the Sisters, with the challenge of physical distances overcome by virtual meetings.

One outcome was the launching of a network called "INTERNATIONAL NETWORK OF GENDER AND SOLIDARITY". Its mission is: "The search for new and effective responses to the situation of women within prostitution, in a globalised world, through strategic thinking and working. It is based in the experience of the Oblatas' Mission projects and aims to establish a continuing information, knowledge and experience exchange globally".

ICA Spain/Empower supported the network's strategic process, which is based on the systematization of their experiences and the development of virtual and face-to-face working styles. The experience started in 2005 and it is still alive - *www.rigys.org* in several languages.

The Oblatas' 1st Global Virtual Encounter in 2006 was facilitated by ICA Spain/Empower. 10 countries were represented from three continents: Africa, America and Europe, and over 120 people attended and participated. Geographically dispersed working groups were formed and their conversations and action points recorded for use by other conference participants, promoting a greater culture of openness and transparency. Ages of participants ranged from 18 to 78 years old.

In 2008 and 2010 the network launched a worldwide virtual campaign against the trafficking of women in the two recent major football events (Germany and S. Africa). Each campaign had over 900 supporters and raised awareness of the phenomenon.

In June 2010, the Oblatas held their first international projects forum. Communities from 5 continents interchanged outcomes, new challenges and planned how to work collectively. This time ICA Spain & Empower were privileged silent witnesses of how the group has empowered itself to maximise the use of web 2.0 technology and a facilitative leadership approach for nurturing their global community.

Interview with Angelica Gomez, Sister and General Secretary of The Oblatas Order of Nuns; carried out on July 13, 2012:

What has working with ICA Spain and Empower meant to you?
"It has given us impetus and a new form of congregational work.

We learned how to optimize the use and appeal of the virtual space. We received training for the coordination and conduct of teamwork for the systematization of our practices and the coaching and mentoring among the Sisters.

The training we received for team work and knowledge of the management of virtual tools allowed us to form a Congregational network, which aimed to facilitate communication between projects, enabled the systematization of the work of the mission. It also allowed the study of prostitution and trafficking of people for purposes of sexual exploitation covering the geographic area where we work.

We are still using and putting into practice what we have learned, noting that it is possible, through this type of interactive communication, to gather for work, prepare meetings, celebrate and promote the fraternity in spite of the geographical distance.

As an Oblata, I am happy and thank you for that time that we used in the past for this learning, which today continues in practice. It facilitates communication, and greater participation is possible. It is accessible to all communities and is saving money.

This experience of using video conferencing is shared with other congregations and we have shown some of them how to use the technology for the purpose of communication.

I would like to continue expanding this knowledge and work to ensure that we continue offering and improving this style of communication and work at the "Congregational level".

Transforming Communities:
ICA Approaches that Work

Ken Hamje

Community Development was unheard of in the integrated communities of the 19th century where local needs were largely met with local creativity, and outside assistance was not expected. But the imbalances in communities created by the industrial revolution and the two world wars created many urban and rural communities with reduced initiative to care for themselves, inviting the emergence of a dependency that has led to today's dominant images of community development as a process of delivering necessary services from "more capable" sources, often from the outside. Now as the 21st century has emerged, it has become clear that there is no bright future for dependent communities, be they urban barrios, suburban bedroom communities or more isolated rural communities. Something radically new is being called for in communities of every continent, region and nation of the world.

In the early 1970's the ICA built the Social Process Triangles which revealed the imbalances in society and the need for viable local communities as the new cradle of social evolution. As previously mentioned in this book, the freedom-giving ToP methods, tens of thousands of participatory Community Forums, and hundreds of demonstration communities were the ICA response towards building viable local communities. From this work and experience a more specific body of methods and practices has emerged which today can be characterized as Community Self-Development.

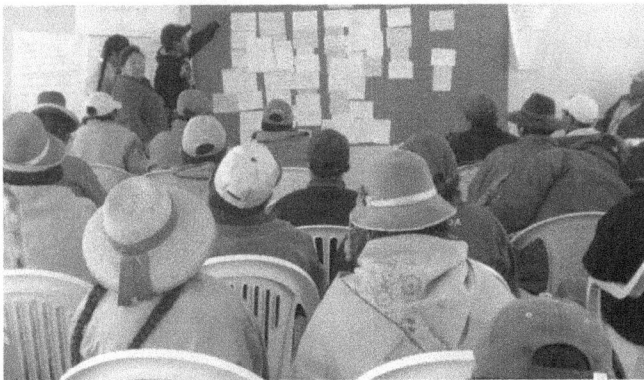

Local leader using ToP methods to lead a consensus-building community meeting.

Typical Community Development Methods

The Community Development approach most widely practiced today is normally built upon a needs-based analysis by professionals from outside the community. Programs or projects are then developed to directly assist in responding to the documented needs, usually with limited input of the local citizens in the delivery process. This approach often leads to immediate improvements in the target needs, but at the same time initiates a dependency on the delivered services which becomes almost impossible to break, and in turn, leads to the demand for ever more intervention to meet ever more community needs. In a world of 7 billion people, this approach simply has no future in the 21st century where it is absolutely essential that ALL the citizens participate in the delivery of necessary services for their communities.

Local needs are typically defined by surveys and analyses conducted by paid professionals from outside of the communities.

LOCAL NEEDS

EXPERT LED PROJECTS

Projects are typically designed and delivered by outside experts to directly meet the needs which they have defined, usually with little community involvement.

The element that is missing in this needs-based approach is taking into account the persistent contradictions that are blocking the natural processes of meeting community needs.

Uniqueness of the ICA approach to Community Development

The ICA approach to community development, employing the ICA developed ToP methods, is dramatically different – in both content and in the style of application.

In the ICA process, the members of the community take the lead, with outside experts acting only as facilitators of the consensus which arises from the will of gathered local people:

- The community <u>makes its own needs assessment</u> – through the group process of defining their commonly held community vision,

- The gathered community then discerns the profound <u>contradictions that are blocking their vision</u> from coming into reality,

- Then the community defines <u>strategic proposals</u> which have the potential to totally eliminate the contradictions that are blocking them,

- And finally, the community makes commitments to <u>implement these proposals</u> at levels which they are currently prepared to support, in order to move themselves forward.

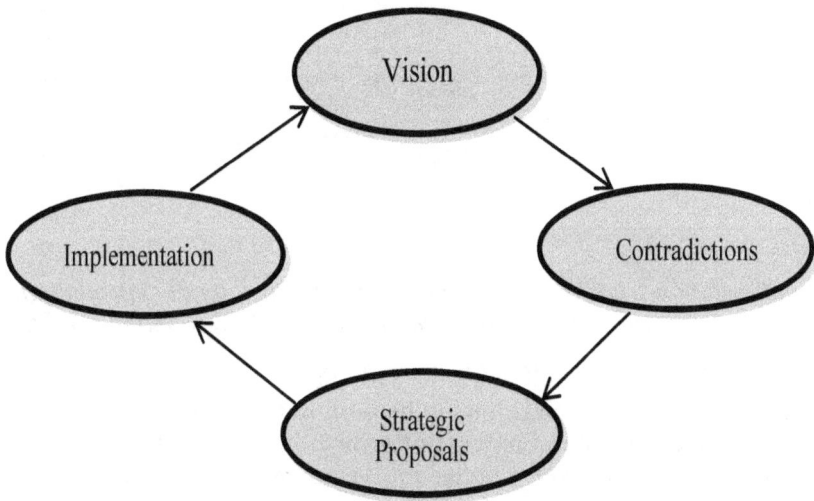

The key to this process is the definition of the Contradictions which, when defined, lead to an immediate breath of relief from the community, like lifting a huge invisible weight from their collective shoulders, for now it is clear to all exactly what needs to be done. For example, in Peru the nearly universal contradiction in communities is the rampant individualism which effectively blocks all forms of cooperation and collaboration. However, once the community ITSELF defines this reality it becomes clear to most of its people that it is essential to begin to work together to change their collective future. This paradigm shift brings clarity about what REALLY needs to be done and is the first step in getting new action taken.

THE CONTRADICTIONS THAT BLOCK THE DEVELOPMENT OF THE COMMUNITIES OF THE HIGH ANDES Prepared by the Institute of Cultural Affairs – ICA-Perú						
INCONGRUENT TRADITIONAL MANAGEMENT OF RESOURCES		LIMITED IMAGES OF THE NECESSITY TO WORK TOGETHER IN COMMUNITY			GAP BETWEEN CAPACITIES AND THE VISION OF THE FUTURE	
INADEQUATE MANAGEMENT OF CAPITAL	STRUCTURES RESTRICT LEADERSHIP	DISTRUST OF FAMILIES TO COLLABORATE	DOMINANCE OF INDIVIDUALISM	LIMITATIONS OF TRADITIONAL ROLES	FRAGMENTED IDENTITY OF THE COMMUNITIES	LIMITED PREPARATION OF THE PEOPLE
- Exit of capital from the communities to purchase products from the outside - Fiestas that last many days and disrupt work patterns - The habit of consuming a lot of alcohol dominates family budgets - Preference to buy new products from outside vendors - Fear of the implications of formalizing family businesses - Dependency on outside sources of capital - Undeveloped disciplines to save money for capital	- Internal rules in each community limit individual initiative - Leadership frozen in rigid structures - Complexity of the requirements of outside actors severely limit local participation - The authorities act without the consensus of the great majority of the population - Authorities live outside of the communities with little knowledge of the realities - Limited management abilities of the authorities - Limited media for local communication	- Traditional conflicts block the collaboration which is necessary today - Little experience with collaboration that is effective - Extreme privacy in family economic affairs blocks collaboration - Family money is in the control of the men - The insecurity caused by frequent thefts undermines the confidence to collaborate - The volunteer community workday is out of style in the new economy of wages - The scarcity mentality justifies the style of not sharing anything with anybody	- Jealousy which denies a neighbor from advancing more than you do - Experiences of many failures with projects requiring community capital - Individualistic groups looking only for their own interests - Profound distrust of people not known personally - Limited communication between families make community development difficult - Conformity style limits the willpower of the people to seek ways for their own development - Little organization of the people to play community roles - Practical neighborhood structures are virtually nonexistent	- The image of leadership is patronizing, self-seeking and macho - The dependency of patronizing structures is the dominant mentality in the zone - The women depend completely on their husbands - Women are not respected if they work to produce income - Only the men speak their thoughts in community meetings - Traditional roles of men, women and youth limit creativity - Youth are not accepted for serious roles in the communities	- Local values have disintegrated with the rapid changes of the new generation - Unfaithfulness of men creates families without a stable economic base - The youth are leaving the communities in search of new opportunities - Outsiders threaten the local identity - Cell phones, Internet and television have replaced traditional cultural events - Tendency to travel to urban centers for the weekend - Vacuum of communal symbols for local identity	- Limited experience with new technologies for economic production - Limited access to new options for making money - The operating vision is out of sync with the local capacities - Limited abilities to read and write - The education level for women is less than of men - The technical training available in the rural areas is focused on urban careers - The population is not prepared to deal with natural disasters

Instituto de Asuntos Culturales (ICA-Perú) 28 de Julio 432, Magdalena del Mar, Lima 17, Perú, (01) 461 0813 – admin@ica-peru.org

A Contradiction Chart is designed to show the Principal Contradiction in the center column, with supporting themes to the left and the right.

Once this process of self-analysis and planning is in action, almost immediately a new vision begins to be born in the people, and soon they find themselves in a spiral process of growth in skills and consciousness as they successively, over months and years, go through the process of Community Self-Development.

We have lived and worked with this process in Peru for over 30 years and have seen hundreds of communities move themselves forward, sometimes quite dramatically and quickly. One of our most memorable experiences was working in Chincha after the 8.0 earthquake in August 2007 where the majority of the people in the city of over 170,000 were homeless and without water or food. Our staff arrived after a few days with essential supplies donated by Japan and there were near riots as each family sought to take as much of the goods as possible. We decided to keep the truck closed up and announced to the crowds that we would return in one hour and distribute goods in their neighborhood, but only if they were ready to cooperate to meet the needs of their neighbors who most needed assistance. Leaders emerged from the crowds, lists were made, goods where distributed in an orderly manner, and there was a new style of cheerfulness and appreciation among the people. We returned to work in this city for over a year with continuing aid from Japan, and even in this extremely difficult situation the people operated with a high level of new-found cooperation and always defined their own needs and took the first action of organizing themselves and displaying initiative before receiving any outside assistance.

Desperate people in Chincha self-organized to receive critically needed water barrels.

Integral Community Development for Sustainability

The focus on the elimination of the underlying contradictions in the community inevitably leads to an awareness of the need for Integral Development if the work in the community is to be sustainable. Tackling the tough challenges is the key to this approach, which takes a focus and seriousness rarely seen in normal sectorial approaches to community development.   How can you expect a sustainable response to early childhood nutrition deficiencies if family incomes are not improved? How can new education initiatives be sustained if there are no jobs or needs for trained youth?   How can you build sustainable communities when new transportation and communication infrastructure lead to an exodus of people and money from the communities? How can any sectorial project bring about sustainable integral development?

Human beings are integral by nature with all genetic, experiential, environmental and emotional influences creating a complex whole which needs to be nurtured at all levels at the same time. Experience has taught us that communities are equally complex and that community development can only be sustainable if it starts from an integral model, not from a hodge-podge of disconnected sectorial projects based on direct needs analysis and dependent on outside expertise and resources. In Peru this is very evident with the huge sectorial social responsibility investments made by the extractive industries which over the years have brought about fragmented dependent communities that systematically send their youth away to the cities for a doubtful future. In recent years, a few of these companies have moved toward an integral development model built upon the formation of teams of local leaders-facilitators who have a vision of making their communities truly viable and sustainable for the 21st Century.

Forming Leaders for Integral Community Development

Leaders of integral community development come in all shapes, sizes, ages and genders but they have at least one thing in common – they have undergone a paradigm shift which allows them to see all people in the community as resources, not as problems. To adopt a cellphone image, these people have undergone a change of "chip" – they simply see life differently. They know that everyone in the community has something of value to contribute and they have a hunger to know what it is and nothing will stop them from getting those contributions recognized by others.

This new breed of volunteer community leader is what we call a "leader-facilitator" – ordinary people who use their skills of facilitation to elicit a new viable future from the citizens who they choose to serve. They share a common understanding that the only secure future for themselves and their families lies in being a contributing member of a cooperative community where collaboration is a way of life that nearly everyone embraces. They are the pioneers who bring about change through their persistent pursuit of the model of an integral community.

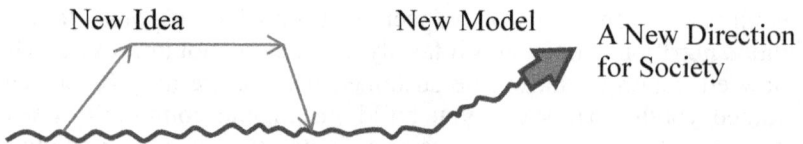

The Pioneer Model for Societal Change

In Peru, each year we train about 300 of these leaders-facilitators to serve about 70 communities using an intensive 6-month leadership formation model for Community Self-Development. We can conduct 10 of these 6-month programs every year with a program staff of ten experienced facilitators, with each program being sponsored by a company to serve about 8-12 communities in their zone of operations. During the first month of the program, two ICA facilitators visit the communities and hold public meetings to orient the people to the program and its benefits, and to assist the communities in selecting their representatives to be trained as facilitators. In total we accept 30 representatives to go to the ICA Training Center in the community of Azpitia, which is the award-winning national demonstration of Community Self-Development started by the ICA in 1979. Here the 30 people spend three very intensive weeks of formation training in the methods and style of facilitation, including a wide range of practical hands-on experiences in agricultural technologies, productive businesses and effective personal and family living. At the end of these 21 days, the changes in these people are quite visible and the testimonials are remarkable.

During the four months following their Azpitia experience, two staff members work for 10 days each month to assist the new leaders to facilitate community meetings, training and demonstration of practical technologies which are immediately usable for the population with no outside assistance. This is Community Self-Development at its finest and the excited residents are invited to join the new leaders in Economic Networks to start new family businesses and increase their family incomes and wellbeing. This combination of enthusiasm and structure, with the support of saving circles for capital formation leads to about 50 new families businesses being initiated by the fourth month of the Implementation phase, putting the communities well on their way toward a new and sustainable future.

Quick Resultsin Canchan. InJuly 2010 we had 30 people from the mountain community of Canchan in our Training Center, and included were three candidates for mayor for the elections in October. During the first week, the three candidates were in constant conflict, each trying to outdo the other with loud and insulting comments, which moderated during the second week as they began to listen to each other. By the third week, the three were seen frequently working together with groups of other interested participants. We found out the following month that the group of 30 participants had decided that only one of the three candidates should run for mayor in order to pool their efforts to put an end to the years of tyranny of the incumbent mayor. In fact, their selected candidate won the election and the district has since moved in a new direction, much to the satisfaction of the citizens and to the amazement of the program sponsor.

The Lever for Sustainable Integral Community Development

After decades of experience with the freeing approach of Community Self-Development, we have learnt that a spark of self-interest is needed to build the momentum of the process to the level of being truly sustainable. We call this spark the lever which lifts the burden of initiating any new process that requires the collaboration of others, and for Community Self-Development that lever is the development of the Local Economy with productive family businesses.

The focus is on supplying the needs of the local economy, for that is where the people have hands-on experience and can know exactly where the market is and what it wants. We avoid programs which create products for outside (global) markets for these sales inevitably need to go through middle-men who have access to the markets and limit the income of the local producers. In addition, these global market sales are subject to great variability and style changes, whereas local economy markets tend to be much more stable with well-known cycles.

If done thoroughly, almost any Local Economy can be very stable and prosperous if it follows these four simple principles of operation:

- Transform local agricultural products for value added (make bread out of wheat)
- Replace products that come from urban factories or China (make school uniforms)
- Create new products and services needed locally (delivery meals for seniors)
- Buy locally made products and services (even if they cost a little more!)

Community Self-Development is Becoming the Future for us All

Incidentally, we will all come to understand that building the Local Economy is not an option in this century –much sooner than we think it will become a matter of survival for us all. As the price of energy climbs sharply – and it will – the "global markets" will dry up as people simply cannot afford to ship vegetables, grains and inexpensive factory goods around the world. LOCAL is the reality of the future, and we are now in the laboratory stage of polishing the models of how it can be done best, as there will be no "big brother" there to help us all when the need is urgent. There simply is not enough money in the world to hire people to replant the watersheds of the world, or even build adequate housing for 7 billion people. These basic tasks of survival have got to be done locally with the creativity and labor of the beneficiaries themselves.

Community Self-Development which engages people in their own care and development is emerging as the only viable future for rural communities in the 21st Century. And what other model can there be for urban communities as well? Already there are over 5,000 local economies in the world that have advanced to the level of having their own local currencies, and many tens of thousands more are in development stages.

LOCAL is the future that is already here. With a current global population of over 7 billion, the task of "community development" is far too large for any public or private institution to handle in any nation. There is no use waiting any longer for assistance – we have but to gather with our neighbors and get to work!

Team work (at 13,400 feet) to prepare the activities for the Implementation phase of the community plan.

Facilitating Asset Based Community Development

Terry D. Bergdall

C ommunity development has been central to the mission of the Institute of Cultural Affairs (ICA) throughout its entire history. This began in the 1960s at 'Fifth City' in the East Garfield Park neighbourhood of Chicago. It continued in the late 1970s an 1980s when ICA created a band of 24 'Human Development Projects' around the world with one being symbolically established in every time zone. Today, independent national ICA organizations are connected in a global federation as members of ICA-International. Their common bond is a shared history and commitment to enabling local community residents to become agents of their own development. ICA has thereby played a pioneering role in re-imaging community development as a participatory bottom-up process.

This is a dramatically different approach in comparison to other conventional practices in poverty alleviation programs that focus on external resources, services, or physical assistance. Hans Hedlund, an Anthropologist at the University of Stockholm, captured this qualitative difference in his study of ICA-Kenya where "staff regarded themselves and their work only as catalysts for community mobilisation by 'facilitating' a process toward equal opportunities and social and economic well-being" (p. 188, Hedlund 2009). ICA's participatory approach has been applied within an overall contextual framework that has since become widely known as "Asset Based Community Development" (ABCD).

Researchers at Northwestern University in Evanston, Illinois, USA, have written extensively on asset-based development within an industrial urban environment (Schmitz 2012; McKnight and Block 2010; Kretzmann and McKnight 1993). Others have adapted and documented the approach in the context of rural villages in the developing 'south' (Mathie and Cunningham 2008). In both, ABCD focuses on the strengths and capacities of local communities. It rests on the conviction that sustainable development emerges from within a community, not from outside, by mobilizing and building upon local resources. In contrast, most conventional development work can be characterized as 'needs-based,' i.e., interventions typically focus on problems and deficiencies. As Kretzmann and McKnight point out, this has the unfortunate effect of encouraging communities to "denigrate themselves" as victims and to put their worst face forward in an effort to attract external assistance (p. 3). It also leads concerned outsiders into becoming charitable 'fixers.' These are not the most effective relationships for enabling long lasting change. Rather than empowering local residents to become agents of their own development, such interventions often have an inadvertent effect of fostering dependency (Chambers 1997).

This chapter examines ways that outsiders, especially in international settings of the 'south,' can play a more creative catalytic role within an asset based-approach. It is a personal reflection drawn from years of first-hand practical experience. What works, what doesn't, what are outstanding issues and questions? They are organised around a number of lessons learned, propositions, examples, and concerns. Though rough and personal, their primary purpose is to share hard-won insights and to prompt others to reflect upon their own experience.

Insiders and outsiders

Most local communities are composed of residents, associations, businesses, and institutions. The African and Asian villages where I've worked have similar aspects as these, though in a simpler form and on a smaller scale than those found in urban areas. The distinction between an insider and outsider in the countryside is more or less obvious: villages consist of local residents with everyone else being an outsider. In para-urban areas that ring major cities, it becomes a little more complex but residency still remains the primary qualifier. Asset-based development means mobilising the skills, resources, and commitment of these residents, along with others grounded in the area, to strengthen the economic and social well-being of the entire community.

Though we would like to have community building 'from the inside out' occur spontaneously, some form of an external stimulus is usually involved. This can often be very minimal. In the Ethiopian highlands, it was exciting to see *kires* (informal funeral associations) initiate small-scale development work on their own after observing the accomplishments of nearby *kires* (see Box 1). But even in such cases, it could be said that the demonstration of successful mobilisation of local assets in one village helped stimulate 'spontaneous' activities in the other. For those interested in *maximising* this effect, major attention is focused on structuring and systematising the *minimal external stimulus* that can effectively occasion significant change across a large number of locations.

Box 1: Stimulants and Spontaneity

An interesting example of the 'dynamics of spontaneity' occurred at the Yilamo *kire* in the Debre Sina District of the Amahara Region. Yilamo residents made plans to improve their main spring during a community planning meeting. The *kire* organised a number of work days and succeeded, as they were proud to report, in "protecting their spring from pollution better than it had ever been done before." The practical result was cleaner water and fewer health problems. This spring was located on the border with another nearby *kire*. When facilitators returned to conduct a follow-up session to the first planning event, some women from the neighbouring *kire* came and asked the Yilamo leaders if they could attend the meeting. They explained that they wanted to use the Yilamo spring because it was much cleaner than the springs in their *kire*; they also said they would like to join in the work to take care of the Yilamo spring. The Yilamo *kire* leaders, however, refused. They told the women to go back to their *kire* and get people to work on cleaning their own spring. The women said that people in their *kire* were not interested in working together like people in Yilamo, so they would not be able to clean their spring in the same way. Still, the *kire* leaders said "this is our spring and should be used only by members of our *kire*." After this dramatic exchange, the women returned home and were eventually successful in cleaning their own spring in a similar manner as at Yilamo.

The form of such an external stimulus is multifaceted with a number of differing dimensions. Beyond individuals from outside of the community who play a 'face-to-face' role there are often various support structures, intermediate organisations, and funding mechanisms. Attention below begins by focusing on the catalytic activities of individuals before considering implications for organisations and structures.

The purpose of a catalyst is to stimulate change

Put simply, the desired change of ABCD is to see more 'building of communities from the inside out.' If one is interested in stimulating change, it is helpful to have a self-conscious framework for understanding how change happens. Since it is foundational to my views about the role of a catalyst, I'll briefly share a theory about change that guides my work. It is based on the writings of Kenneth Boulding (1956).

Behaviour, the way people act individually or within a group, is based on the way they see themselves in the world. It's a matter of self-perception, self-story, self-image – which are all ways of saying the same thing. For example, it could be said that the unilateral tendencies and actions of the current US government are consistent with an image of rugged American individualism. Images are created through the reception of 'messages.' People continually incorporate, or discard, new messages into their accumulated understanding of themselves in the world. Messages come in many forms: verbal, visual, and experiential. Education is an elaborate process of conveying various 'messages' about particular subjects. Messages come in varying degrees of strength: one reads all the time about the negative health effects of fatty foods. Yet these often only mildly alter one's prevailing self-understanding and behavioural choices about diet. A heart attack, however, is a much stronger message – as are most experiential messages.

Images go through a continual process of change. Most involve minor adjustments as new pieces of information (messages) are aligned to an existing image. Inconsistent messages that challenge a strong image are usually ignored. Sometimes, especially if received several times from differing sources, or if the message is strongly experiential, 'doubt' begins to emerge as the contradictory messages gain prominence. Radical change occurs when an established image is replaced by a totally new self-understanding. When images change, behaviour changes. This understanding about change can be summarised in five points: 1) people live out of images, 2) images control behaviour, 3) images are created by messages, 4) images can change, and 5) when images change, behaviour changes.

The desired change in my work has been to shift community self-understanding from *passivity* (e.g., waiting as 'clients' to receive services; self-images of being 'victims') to becoming *active agents* of their own development.

Catalysts play the role of a facilitator, not a direct implementer.

Effective catalysts from outside of the community don't do anything directly *for* people. They encourage people to do things are their own. ABCD emphasises that one leads best by stepping back. Communities drive their own development; catalysts facilitate the process. This implies a number of practical activities that are far easier to talk about than to do.

Catalysts enable a community to look realistically at itself. They hold up a mirror so residents can see themselves as they really are. Because people have been well conditioned to focus on their problems, facilitators emphasize analytic tools and exercises that help community residents to *identify and recognize strengths and capacities* which they may have overlooked or ignored in the past. Asset mapping tools developed by ABCD are valuable in doing this. Other methods from other sources are also helpful for identifying local strengths and capacities, e.g., those known under the name of 'participatory rural appraisal' (PRA) are widespread in the 'south.' Key to them all, however, is a basic principle: Catalysts do not do the mapping, they facilitate community residents to map assets for themselves.

Catalysts *connect* people with each other and their existing resources. In doing so, they emphasize inclusiveness. Everyone in a community has something to contribute, be they at the centre of the community or on its margins. Facilitators, therefore, are leery of working only with small representational groups of 'leaders.' This often requires catalysts to play a role of 'provocateurs' because small cliques of leaders are typically quite content to assume responsibility themselves on behalf of the community at large. (More on a provocateur below.)

Catalysts facilitate the community to *affirm its real situation* without illusions or false hopes. It has been my experience that no matter how much a facilitator might focus discussions on a community's assets (i.e., the half glass that is full), sooner or later local people insist that the conversation turn to needs and problems (i.e., the glass is half empty). Though foremost attention is focused on assets, an over reluctance to discuss problems is a subtle denial of the real situation. The 'problem' with discussing problems is that they quickly cause a community to turn its attention outside of itself. Local frustrations are blamed on others or solutions are seen as being dependent upon external realities or generosities. A sense of victimisation is reinforced rather than challenged. Affirming the real situation means acknowledging the active participation of a community in the problem. When a community recognises how it contributes to creating or perpetuating a problem, it also reveals practical ways that they themselves can self-consciously address that problem (see Box 2). Resolution may not be complete, but a way forward is always possible.

Box 2: **Examining the Situation from Within**

Discussions about local assets during the planning meeting were interesting to people in Endabeg, a village in the Babati District of Tanzania, but they also wanted facilitators to consider their needs. Q: 'Okay, what do you think are some of your biggest needs?' A: 'We need for the co-op to deliver sufficient amounts of fertilizers to us on a timely basis.' Q: 'What is the problem that you hope will be solved?' A: 'Our crop production continues to go down every year.' Q: 'Besides your concerns about fertilizer, what are other possible reasons for the drop in crop production?' A: 'We are losing top soil to erosion.' Q: 'What practices are you following in Endabeg that might be perpetuating these problems? A1: 'We are cutting trees on the high slopes above the fields; water is running too fast and flows over our fields.' A2: 'We are not careful about the direction in which we plow our fields.' A3: 'It isn't a soil erosion issue, but we are always planting the same crop year after year so the ground is getting tired.' Q: 'What can you do differently in Endabeg to address some of these problems that are contributing to the ongoing drop in your crop production?' A: 'We could create small terraces, we could replant trees above our fields, we could rotate our crops, we could build some small damns to slow down the running water during the rains, we could ..., we could ... etc, etc. (Note: It takes patience and skill for a facilitator to ask probing questions in different ways; it also takes time to explore and consider different ideas and suggestions; small group work can be helpful here.)

Having identified its assets, catalysts facilitate people to build *practical plans of action* for mobilizing their resources and accomplishing realistic objectives. Local development plans thus become a symbol of consensus and a rallying point for inclusive action. They also give a practical foundation of any organizational issues that might arise within a community. My personal bias for being a catalyst is on enabling quick action rather than on long preparations periods for gathering detailed information and analysing it (whether on assets or other). In my experience, people learn best by doing and then *reflecting upon the experience*. The sooner people begin acting on something of substance (even simple activities can be substantial), the better. Key, of course, is local residents being the primary implementers of their own plans. Catalysts are cautious about playing a direct and overly active role in connecting local communities with outside resources. The basic principle is this: don't do anything for people that they can do themselves.

Catalysts embody a 'presence' that helps build trust

As a university intern living and working on the west side of Chicago in the late sixties, scathing reference to 'limousine social workers' made a strong impression on me. More than simply describing those who drove in from the warm comforts of the suburbs to help needy people in the inner city (the 'ghetto' as we spoke back then), it symbolised an inauthentic relationship. Sophomoric abstractions about 'bad faith' suddenly became very real to me as I wrestled with my own vocation. Creating a genuine relationship with local people is essential for outsiders if they are to effectively play a catalytic role, but how is it practically done? The answer probably lies more in the way one actively struggles with the question than in prescribing a definitive formula. During the meeting in Evanston, we heard about work in Bosnia and an outsider embodying a genuine 'presence' to the local situation.

Though maybe not definitive guidelines, there are factors that might lead one in a helpful direction. Catalysts are *accountable* to local communities. They are there, in some form or another, only at the invitation of the community. But as outsiders, they are upfront about their role and intentions so everyone in can see their purpose and understand their motives. In doing so, a creative sense of 'obedience' to the community is established. Catalysts are consistent: they do what they say they are going to do. They are transparent: they are forth-coming about their actions and are open to being questioned about them.

Outsiders are not insiders. There may be examples where outsiders have become insiders through a lifetime of commitment (often with significant personal sacrifice), but anything short of this probably means that outsiders will always remain distinct from the community. Even in relatively short-term engagements, however, a foundation for trust can built through the integrity of one's empathetic respect and *'shared austerity.'* It means standing genuinely present to the local situation. This is intimately tied to the subtle communication of visual, verbal, and experiential messages. During preparations for launching the 'Community Empowerment Programme' in Ethiopia, this issue was faced directly. Facilitators began to see how many of their own ways of acting needed to change if they were going to be effective in working with the rural population. 'Shared austerity' in that context meant personal participation in many of the practical hardships experienced day in and day out by local community residents (see Box 3).

Box 3: Shared Austerity

One long session during preparations in Ethiopia dealt with ways that villagers typically perceive government workers. It was generally agreed that it was one of mistrust and suspicion. Group reflections took place around the following questions: What behaviour reveals mistrust? What images are consistent with that way of acting? What experiences might have helped create those images? If trust is an important factor for working successfully with villagers, what does this tell us about how we should carry out facilitation activities?

Conversation turned to travel modes of the villagers with whom they would be working – which consisted of walking along highland paths or riding donkeys and mules. There was near rebellion when the idea was first suggested that the facilitators do the same instead of traveling by four-wheel drive vehicles. Agreement was only reached to try it on the first workshops and then to 'evaluate' its impact. The experience was a life-changing event for most of them: their interaction with villagers was at a depth they had never before known. Henceforth, the facilitators willingly took on severe hardships in conducting *kire* workshops. They traveled for hours by 'public means' to the distant districts (i.e., in the back of open lorries in dust and rain), walked or rode mules for miles over harsh terrain to reach designated *kires*, and had slept in the flea infested homes of peasant farmers for several weeks. This was a dramatic change for both villagers and young government professionals alike. Though not complete by itself, it did help to shift the relationship dramatically in the direction of mutual respect.

Catalysts have an agenda.

Those interested in ABCD want to see community development driven by the community. Outside catalysts are interested in providing minimal stimulus to overcome inertia and build momentum. They facilitate the process and avoid becoming a direct implementer. They are not the primary actors – those roles belong to members of the community. ABCD catalysts and facilitators, however, are not neutral. They have a definite agenda based on a coherent strategy with real aims. Without one, activities like asset mapping, etc., are reduced to being a series of rudderless techniques.

Effective catalysts, I believe, are bold in declaring their agenda. Important messages can easily be missed when conveyed in a timid manner. This, of course, doesn't mean that one should indulge oneself as an obnoxious dogmatist, but it does mean acting with clarity and consistency while remaining politely firm. Integrity, which is the raw basis for trust, comes hand in hand with the transparent declaration of one's own agenda.

Women's participation in rural Africa is a good example of an outsider's agenda. The strategic justification for involving women is the inclusive widening of the circle so that all assets within a community can be recognised and drawn upon. In African cultures, however, involving women in the planning and management of important economic and social matters is almost always an imposition from the outside. It is sometimes unwelcome and at times overtly resented. This is one mirror that many male leaders would just as soon not be held to their face. By insisting upon women's participation in strong patriarchal societies, a catalyst moves away from the congenial impressions associated with a 'neutral' facilitator and dashes headfirst in the direction of a provocateur or an agitator. The challenge is to play these roles respectfully while also remaining resolutely committed to the importance of a well considered strategy (see Box 4). The specific features of a strategy may vary depending upon differing circumstances, but an effective catalyst conveys them clearly and acts accordingly.

Box 4: **Facilitation and Transparency**

During preparations for the programme in Ethiopia, the facilitators said it would be difficult to have women and youth involved in planning community development activities; 'it's not in the culture of the highlands.' As with the transportation issue, we decided to give it an initial try during the first community planning events and then reflect on the experience. These first two were held in kires near to Dessie in South Wollo. Set-up work was done by facilitators who explained that the purpose of the planning, including the importance of women's involvement.

On the appointed day, I hiked with the facilitators to the first kire where we were greeted by a large number of men waiting for the workshop to begin. Those present easily represented 90% of the kire's 60 or so households, but no women were to be seen. When asked about the women, the kire chairman said 'we speak for our women here.' All eyes of the facilitators turned to me while silently saying 'we told you so.' I repeated the standard line – women's involvement is important for engaging and drawing upon all of the strengths and resources within the community. Once again we were told that women would not be allowed to attend. 'I understand your position' I replied, 'and I hope you understand ours. If women don't participate in the planning, we cannot stay and facilitate the process.' With that we thanked them for their time and hiked back to Dessie.

Word in rural Africa can spread like wildfire. When we arrived in the second neighbouring kire a few days later, an acceptable quorum of women was present (about 30) along with a number of young people (admittedly, they were all young boys, not girls, but a catalyst is always ready to be flexible!). Small groups of women, youth, and men met to discuss strengths of the community and to suggest ideas about things that could be done in the community through the use of their own resources.. A good substantial plan of small-scale simple 'infrastructure' projects were planned (i.e., a small check damn to control erosion, terracing on some problematic fields, and protection of the spring). In closing reflections, several men said they didn't know before that 'their' women had so many good practical ideas.

Community planning workshops with over 300 similar kires were held during the next three years in South Wollo. Never again was it necessary to cancel one because of insufficient women's participation. This probably had more to do with the facilitators' personal commitment to the agenda of the program, and the manner in which they presented it, than with anything else.

Leveraging external resources.

Most development programmes in Africa are dominated by a 'needs' perspective. There is often an overly eager desire among outsiders, even among those who talk a good line about 'bottom-up' development and 'local capacity building,' to rush quickly into arranging financial and material support for local communities. At some point it probably is important for most local communities to leverage external resources to complement their own. An effective catalyst, however, is extremely cautious: the premature arrival of external sources can overwhelm local efforts. Special attention should be given to the word 'leveraging.' It implies the community is the driving force for finding and obtaining additional resources. 'Introducing' or 'providing' imply that the essential initiating actor is outside of the community.

Like most things in an asset-based approach, the appropriate timing for leveraging external resources depends upon particular circumstances. It is yet another important factor in the development of a coherent strategy for guiding catalytic action. It has been my experience that it is usually more effective to delay major attention on external resources. If uncertain about timing, it is better to error on the side of later rather than sooner. The reason for this has to do with perceptions and self-images within the community. The image of being a 'needy client' is often a deeply entrenched one. It causes people to look first outside of themselves for solutions to problems. Communities experience internal power by mobilising their own resources. The more times they successfully repeat it, the stronger the experiential messages become for reinforcing a new image (i.e., we are agents of our own development) to replace an old dominant one (i.e., we are needy clients). Forming a new image – which is the foundation for change – is a delicate process. Emerging new images are easily overpowered by old familiar messages (see Box 5 below).

Box 5: Unintended Results

The "Cooperative Members Participation Programme" (CMPP) in east Africa was a strategic effort (via funding from the Swedish Cooperative Centre, Utan Gräsner), to transform local co-ops from being service providers to becoming organisational vehicles for local initiative and action based upon local resources. A small team of two or three facilitators would work with a village co-op to enable the creation of a local development plan. Facilitation of the planning, and then follow-up to assist in the review and adjustment of these plans, were the only external support offered by the programme: absolutely no material or financial resources were available through CMPP.

One of the first of these workshops was held with a village co-op near Kilosa in the Morogoro Region of Tanzania. During the workshop, villagers decided to finally complete construction of a small 'clinic' -- a simple 20 square metres building so that village women would have a place to go to give birth in a sanitary environment and rest for a few days afterwards. Construction on the building had begun two years earlier when UNICEF provided a small grant to the village for this purpose. The money, however, had run out before the building was completed: it had stood half finished ever since as the village waited for UNICEF to return with more money. It was decided during the meeting to make the clinic a top priority (the idea was brought to the fore by a large number of women, many of whom were attending a village planning meeting for the first time). Shortly afterwards, they organised the making of mud bricks, completed the walls, and made wooden shutters for empty windows. When a national cooperative officer happened to visit the village a few weeks later, the villagers explained that they were close to finishing the building: next week they were going to remove old rusting tin sheets from a collapsed co-op storage shed to complete the clinic by laying the roof. The official was extremely impressed with the way people were working together and using their own meagre resources to accomplish things. To support and encourage their efforts, he told them that his organisation would buy the village new roofing sheets so there was no need for them to use the old rusting ones. The villagers cancelled their workday anticipating the arrival of the new metal sheets. Unfortunately, the official could not make good on his commitment and the materials never arrived. When the facilitators returned to the village three months later to conduct a progress review on the village development plan, the clinic remained unfinished and was beginning to deteriorate once again.

Mini-grants as the 'leading' catalytic strategy and its relationship to face-to-face facilitation

This is certainly not an either/or issue. After three and a half years of work in Ethiopia, the primary proposal from those us who worked closest with the 'Community Empowerment Programme' was to establish 'District Development Funds' that would manage and oversee mini-grants to local *kires*. Though funding for this was not secured (so it never happened), it does seem an appropriate complement to face-to-face facilitation – especially in the more mature stages of a strategy based on face-to-face interactions.

Because of my limited experience with community foundations, I have questions about using mini-grants as a *leading*, or initiating, catalytic strategy (i.e., without much face-to-face catalytic interaction). This is especially true in Africa. My questions are primarily concerned with other ways of nurturing a 'learning environment' within local communities. The practical skills and institutional infrastructure of rural villages in Africa are far different from those found in North America. I would like to personally learn more about different experiences of community foundations in the 'south.' I would especially like to learn more from Latin America where I have no experience at all. What practical mechanisms have they found for enabling a learning environment to occur in the absence of the face-to-face interaction. Or am I being too narrow in my thinking with the assumption that mini-grants strategies are overly constrained (at least in the early stages of proposal writing and project formation) by paper interactions? Clearly, these are edge questions in my own learning process.

How long should an outsider be involved in the catalytic process?

In Africa, I have favoured quickly moving into action without overly long preparation stages of data gathering and analysis. The emphasis has been on structuring and systematising the minimal external stimulus that can effectively occasion significant change within a large number of communities. These are clearly aspects of a *broad expansive strategy* for catalysing change. This is sharp contrast to a more *in-depth intensive strategy* that focuses on a smaller number of communities – perhaps as small as one. The intention among intensive strategies is to widely influence other communities through the power of their demonstration. Expansive strategies imply more brief engagement over shorter periods of time while intensive strategies imply lengthy involvement over the long haul. Indeed, it seems that within an intensive strategy, if involved for a truly long time, an outsider almost loses one's identity as such and becomes more or less a member of the community. Their immersion is a confirmation of vocational commitments manifest in where they live and how they work.

Neither strategy is better than the other, but they are different. Playing the role of an external catalyst is an art and not a science. There is no one 'right' way to do it. Forming a particular coherent strategy depends upon aligning a range of factors within the local context. The big issue, I'd suggest, is consistency and transparency in making the alignment. To summarise my experience, the structure of a bare bones 'minimal external stimulus' of an expansive strategy working with several communities in near proximity (e.g., a district) might look like this:

1) An initial meeting with established local leaders in their home villages to discuss the idea of doing development based on local resources; a contextual discussion about expanding inclusiveness via gender and age in the planning and management; agreement (or not) to host a community planning event and clarifying preparation issues.
2) A two-day community-wide planning event that identifies key assets and creates local action plans based on the connection and utilisation of local resources.
3) Four quarterly community-wide 'review' meetings where progress reports are given, physical inspections are made, and everyone at the meeting is engaged in reflections about lessons learned; this is followed by preparation of action plans for the next quarter.
4) At least one district-wide meeting during the course of the year where representatives of communities and government officials come together to celebrate local accomplishments, share ideas about accelerating the process, and draw together lessons learned about bottom-up development.
5) Regular learning events (at least quarterly) for outsider catalysts to meet together, share their experience, reflect upon lessons learned, and make modifications for their next steps of interaction with local communities.

Since I have worked with several programmes along these lines over the years, I am always asked about long-term change within this 'minimalist' approach. Though short-term effects are modest, I believe them to be significant. While I have extensively studied many communities in the short-term (e.g., I followed activities in two Tanzanian villages through annual visits over a three-year period – the cases are available to those interested), I, too, am curious about long-term change. Now, with the passage of several years, it would be valuable to visit those same two villages in Tanzania again (or some of the *kires* in Ethiopia) and learn what has happened since.

How do outsiders learn to become catalysts?

An environment for mutual learning is crucial. The environment (participants in attendance, location for site visits, a participatory format) is as important as the composition of topics to be considered. Since there is no one right way to be a catalyst, the more diversity of experience and perspective the better. When I have facilitated such events, I've structured time and participatory exercises around subjects that allow for a lot of interaction and group reflection. Contextual frameworks are provided primarily to stimulate conversation and creative thinking. Good topics and exercises for enabling outsiders to learn about catalytic action might include:

- how does change occur?
- what happens to a community when it focuses on assets? what happens to a community when it focuses on needs? how is the difference between the two informative to someone who desires to be a catalyst?
- site visits to successful examples of an ABCD approach.
- a review of various facilitation techniques; practical experience of using such techniques.
- designing engagement plans for catalytic action in the group members' home situations.
- sharing and reflection (and creative critique and feedback from others).
- lessons learned about funding and leveraging external resources.
- what are the most appropriate ways for an outsider to enter a community? what is a genuine 'invitation' (and what isn't)?
- what lessons have been learned about what an effective catalyst does and does not do?

In making this list, I realise that these are the 'hot topics' that I personally want to explore! Which is appropriate since learning is at its strongest when it is a shared experience and a lifetime pursuit. It does offer an insight, however, for designing any learning event: topics and exercises, etc., are tailored around the interests and questions of the particular people who have come together to learn.

What lessons can be offered to intermediary organisations in the effective design and management of ABCD-oriented activities?

For those of us who are working within an ABCD context, there is an inherent skepticism to interventions designed, managed, and controlled by organisations outside of a local community. Most have been fostered within a needs perspective and treat community residents like clients. Social service agencies, municipal governments, united ways, and various humanitarian organisations have sprung from this tradition and are susceptible to its perpetuation. In many ways ABCD is an alternative defined over against this perspective. In the 'south,' non-governmental organisations (NGOs) have emerged as a major presence in the social development landscape. While they are not the only form of intermediate organisations working in the field of community development, they are a dominant one.

Problems and criticisms are as easy to list for intermediary organisations in the 'south' as they are elsewhere. The project orientation of their work is usually short-term: it feeds upon problem identification and a quick fix. They are accountable primarily to donors, board of directors, or other external authorities – and not, in the first instance, to the people they serve. It is in their self-interest to remain problem-focused because it secures their own role as problem solvers. Many NGOs, accordingly, have begun to closely resemble businesses that hawk their wares (i.e., services), and in doing so provide ongoing employment for their professional staff. In regards to packaging their projects and programmes, there is a strong tendency to co-opt fashionable sexy language -- and ABCD can easily become one -- without substantially changing practices that perpetuate the professional-client relationship. As one recent book points out, many have turned the creative insights of 'participation' into a new tyranny (Cook and Kothari 2002). There are times when 'lords of poverty' isn't much of an exaggeration (Handcock 1989).

Though it is easy to see a glass half empty, it is also possible to find and build upon the assets of NGOs and other intermediary organisations. Though actual practice may lag far behind the rhetoric that these groups commonly use about community-based development, many individuals within these organisations have a genuine vision to which they aspire. Through them, there is an opportunity for an ABCD faculty to enable wider institutional learning to occur.

Within any particular intermediary organisation, this means holding up a mirror and letting it reveal naked realities. The selection below is a 'mirror' that I held up to a programme in Zambia (see Box 6). It served as the central reference point for a two-day workshop with staff and senior management of the NGO. Admittedly, deep discussions in learning environments like this don't immediately overcome complex contradictions. After all, the 'mirror' revealed structural flaws as well as issues in daily practice. But they can call forth new perspectives that encourage and enrich personal convictions. Besides altering practices in the present, it may also lead toward different ways of approaching community building in the future. A major challenge is to engage donors in a similar learning process for it is they who often have an extremely influential role in establishing overall frameworks. Publications and documentation of good examples of 'building communities from the inside out' is obviously another way that the dialogue can be intensified.

Box 6: Mixed Messages

The Programme of Support for Poverty Elimination (PROSPECT) in Zambia gives an example of an inadvertent gap between rhetoric and practice. This multi-million pound project is funded by the British government and implemented by CARE. Its objective is the alleviation of poverty and improved household livelihoods in the para-urban 'slums' of Lusaka through locally planned and initiated projects. Capacity building of community institutions is a central part of the entire programme and PRA techniques have been used throughout its operation. In the first instance, it is not a typical intervention with a focus on a particular sector but it does include provisions for funding infrastructure projects selected by the community. It is intended that local capacity building and organizational development should take place around these inputs. More often than not the infrastructure development desired by the community is an improvement in water supply.

Yet 'mixed signals' are caused by an emphasis on bottom-up development and local capacity-building on one hand and the completion of large infrastructure projects on the other. They lead to immense confusion and conflict in regards to community participation, ownership, and service. Community residents with whom PROSPECT works are told that they are the 'owners' of the water project but soon discover that the municipal water company is really the 'legal' owner while the community is merely the 'symbolic' owner. They are told that ongoing 'sustainable' development can only occur through local initiatives, and the labour spent on water construction should therefore be voluntary, but previous work within the programmme's immediate predecessor (which was also implemented by CARE) was paid with 'food for work.' In planning implementation schedules and work plans, community residents discover conditions and externally imposed deadlines.

When such 'blended' approaches are employed (combining traditional 'blueprint' projects with open-ended 'process' programmes), even when the ultimate intention declared in programme documents is empowerment and local capacity building, 'external management' during the phases of project implementation, to one degree or another, is a very difficult problem to overcome. Handovers in ownership clearly imply transfers. People may be consulted and given a role to play in various phases of a project's life through actively seeking their participation in one form or another; this may include the use of PRA techniques. Ultimately, however, authority for such projects resides outside of the community and is largely governed by interests of external agencies. Though characterization of 'external management' may be seen as a harsh judgment by NGOs like CARE (especially within participatory capacity-building programmes like PROSPECT), introduction of major infrastructure projects greatly enhances the potential risks of externally determined objectives that must be fulfilled in one way or another. This external agenda greatly influences, or even drives, the process, regardless of how enlightened programme intentions may be.

What practical advice might be offered to intermediary organisations in the 'south?' A good approach begins with a good design. Good here essentially means 'consistent.' The gap between rhetoric and practice usually arises when a programme design attempts to 'blend' approaches. Historically, needs-based approaches have attempted to do things *for* people. There is a lot of discussion today about doing development *with* people. An asset-based approach emphasises development *by* people themselves. Blended approaches are a result of cut-and-paste efforts to marry together activities from two or more of these approaches. The primary contradiction for most community-based programmes, I believe, is one of *mixed messages*. Blending approaches creates a structural recipe that virtually ensures confusion. Good intermediary organisations strive to identify these contradictions and work very hard to alleviate mixed messages wherever they might creep in. Ultimately, this is where the integrity of an outside catalyst is truly at stake; this is also where an external catalyst is most vulnerable.

Conclusion

There is an academic tendency to focus on detailed categories by breaking things down into manageable parts. My reflections above have done just that. Being an effective facilitator and catalyst, however, is an artful matter of aligning actions into a holistic, unified undertaking. May those of us who have a passion for empowering community residents through an asset-based approach continue to learn from each other about the effective orchestration of the whole.

References

Boulding, K., (1956), *The Image: Knowledge in Life and Society*, The University of Michigan Press, Ann Arbor.

Cook, B., and Kothari, U. (2002), *Participation: the New Tyranny?*, Zed Books, London.

Chambers, R., (1997), *Whose Reality Counts: Putting the First Last*, Intermediate Technology, London.

Handcock, G. (1989), *The Lords of Poverty: The Power, Prestige, and Corruption of the International Aid Business*, Macmillian, London.

Hedlund, H., (2009), "From Mission to Profession: A Narrative of the Institute of Cultural Affairs" in *Ethnographic Practice And Public Aid: Methods and Meanings in Development Cooperation*, Hagberg, S., and Widmark, C. (editors), Uppsala University.

Kretzmann J., and McKnight, J. (1993), *Building Communities from the Inside Out: A Path Toward Finding and Mobilizing a Community's Assets*, Institute for Policy Research, Evanston.

Mathie, A., and Cunningham, G. (editors), (2008), *From Clients to Citizens: Communities changing the course of their own development*, Practical Action (UK).

McKnight, J., and Block, P. (2010), *The Abundant Community: Awakening the Power of Families and Neighborhoods*, Berrett-Koehler Publishers, San Francisco.

Schmitz, P. (2012), *Everyone Leads: Building Leadership and Community from the Bottom Up*, Wiley, San Francisco.

Accelerating Sustainability in Chicago's 77 Communities - A Working Case Study

Edited by Karen Snyder Troxel

---

*This is a "working" case, describing the first year of ICA-USA: Chicago's **Accelerate 77** program being implemented in 2011-2015. Compiled and edited on behalf of the ICA from various sources for the purpose of sharing with others interested in initiating such an effort.*

The Institute of Cultural Affairs (ICA) experience in comprehensive community development began 50 years ago in Chicago's 5th City neighborhood of East Garfield Park in Chicago. After ten years of working in 5th City as a pilot, human development project, 24 other projects were replicated in rural villages and urban neighborhoods in every time zone around the world. ICA has since operated in 32 nations globally.

In 2011 as Chicago staff and colleagues began anticipating ICA's 50-year anniversary, the decision was made that the celebration of the past would be focused on the future – the next 50 years – with an emphasis on serving *environmental and social justice issues* in Chicago's communities. Paul Hawken[1] was helpful in revealing that there is enormous energy and response to these twin global issues that are largely unrecognized.

As ICA began to assess Chicago's needs for empowering sustainable communities, it became apparent that in Chicago too there are myriad responses to social and environmental needs, generally unrecognized and relatively isolated, and with limited interaction among them. At the same time many organizations, foundations, companies, and government agencies have programs and resources to assist local sustainability efforts, with communities unaware of the opportunities or unfamiliar with ways to access them.

Therefore ICA decided to mark its 50th Anniversary with a five-year plan to acknowledge and support responsive and effective work happening

---

1. In his book, Blessed Unrest: How the largest movement in the world came into being and why no one saw it coming (2007)

in every one of Chicago's 77 communities. Coordinating a three-phase project: "Accelerating Green Initiatives in Chicago's 77 Community Areas" (known as *Accelerate 77*), ICA intends to expand environmental sustainability activities at the community level.

The underlying strategy is to *identify* current sustainability initiatives in all of Chicago's 77 community areas; *connect* them with one another to inspire new ideas, practices and motivation through peer interchange; and *engage* residents in systematic learning, planning, and collective action. It is anticipated that the project will *accelerate* environmental sustainability in a bottom-up fashion driven by practical action, expanded imagination and greater organizational capacities among local groups.

Phase I: IDENTIFY
August 2011 – August 2012

ICA launched the first year by sponsoring an initiative to research and document successful sustainable projects in every one of Chicago's 77 communities. Working with universities and colleges, ICA developed a documentation process, involving students doing community interviews and asset mapping, to identify community sustainability initiatives in all 77 areas of the city. Professors from Chicago State, DePaul, Northeastern Illinois, Loyola and Roosevelt involved entire classes in the research.

Over 180 students were engaged in identifying sustainable initiatives in 55 of the 77 communities between August 2011 and June 2012. Students will research the remaining 22 during the summer program.

I COMMUNITY ENGAGEMENT
Task:
- Ensure initial identification of green initiatives
- Reviewing community initiatives documentation
- Neighborhood outreach and engagement to facilitate initiative selection

Deliverables:
- Initiatives identified in all Chicago's 77 communities
- Organized document of all initiatives identified
- Clear process for initiative selection
- Three initiatives selected by each of the 77 communities

II COMMUNICATIONS AND PROMOTION
Tasks:
- Promotional plan that includes the message, target audiences, and creative outreach to a diverse demographic
- Maintain communication and engagement through social media and email blasts
- Manage digital content and media needs, including community documentation, the program website, photography, and portable media, developing or soliciting new content as necessary

Deliverables:
- Comprehensive communications plan
- Engaged virtual community
- Critical content posted on the website
- Accelerate 77 results in a publicly accessible format

III EVENT DESIGN AND IMPLEMENTATION
Tasks:
- Planning and implementing event logistics (e.g., equipment list, in-kind calls, food plan)
- Strategizing how to make the event green

Deliverables:
- Logistics plan for prep of the city-wide share fair on September 15, 2012
- Timeline and implementation of logistics
- Space design

Documentation of all the initiatives is being posted on a newly developed website scheduled to be formally launched in June 2012. This site will incorporate web-based social networking tools with state-of-the art asset mapping tools to create an interactive medium that will connect and engage sustainability stakeholders citywide.

Accelerate 77 is hosting a ten-week ICA Summer Internship Program for 40 students to complete the research, document it and plan and implement the September 15th Share Fair. Interns will have the option of involvement in one of the three work arenas described in the right-hand column of this page.

There are three cycles in the internship program. This allows the program to be flexible to the students' needs for credit hours and part-time jobs. In Cycle I (May 28-June 15) interns interested in advanced leadership development will have three weeks orientation and training. Then they will have hands-on experience of co-leading teams in the three areas throughout Cycles II and III.

Similarly, Cycle II is of three weeks (June 18-July 6) and Cycle III is of four weeks (July 9-August 3). Participants will have the option of participating in both Cycles II and III for seven-weeks – or alternatively choosing one of the two Cycles. The time commitment is a minimum of twenty hours per week.

Phase II: CONNECT
September 15 - December 2012

The second phase is going to be launched with a one-day **"Sharing Approaches That Work"** conference **September 15, 2012** that highlights neighborhood innovations in clean energy, waste reduction, green jobs, recycling, local food production, etc. The day will act as a "share fair" for community representatives to learn from one another while attending a series of "connection seminars" during which supportive organizations will present opportunities for accelerating green initiatives through various resources available to neighborhoods. The share fair "kick-off" will welcome attendees with a keynote address from a prominent leader in the environmental movement.

Sharing Approaches that Work community interaction to learn from each other's experiences	Keynote Address	Connection Seminars presentation by resource organizations on grant and program opportunities

The conference will be an opportunity for creating a path forward in Chicago's neighborhoods built upon current innovations from local residents. The conference will showcase resources from organizations like Illinois Clean Energy Community Fund, Growing Power, Faith in Place, The Delta Institute, ComEd, Center for Neighborhood Technology (CNT), Transition Chicago as well as the City of Chicago and the State of Illinois.

A report on the 77 neighborhood sustainable initiatives will document successful local undertakings and key lessons learned in their implementation. A summary report will document the event, the attendees, summaries of each organization and seminar topics, will be created and distributed to attendees and stakeholders citywide. Video clips and summary notes from each seminar will be made available online. The extent and scope of connections made, the value of knowledge, resources and tools shared, the effectiveness of best practices that emerged and outstanding challenges as yet unmet will be distributed. Connections and documentation from the forum will inform the launch of Phase III. These will be shared electronically with neighborhoods and nonprofit organizations across Chicago.

Phase III: ENGAGE
January 2013- December 2015

The anticipated result will be multiple local initiatives that will significantly contribute to the success of the Chicago Climate Action Plan by 2020. We envision creating many alliances with partners in the work of building sustainable resilient Chicago communities

The **"Sharing Approaches that Work"** conference will help encourage and accelerate local efforts while catalyzing follow-up work in Chicago's 77 neighborhoods. ICA will facilitate a process of systematic learning, planning, and collective action drawing upon initiative documentation, social network website activity, organization feedback, and forum activities. In the next three years, local efforts through networking, planning and training workshops, local share fairs, and new collaborative relationships between neighborhood groups and stakeholders citywide will accelerate the impact of local environmental sustainability work.

While much can be planned through lessons learned during Phase I and Phase II, many details of Phase III will be informed by the innovation, best practices, and leadership that emerges organically through continued engagement. The ability to recognize these emerging assets and facilitate their application is critical and fundamental to the culmination of success with the project. ICA's long history and experience in facilitation, consensus building, and community development will guide collaborative activities and nurture this emergence over time.

As a complement to this organic process across all of Chicago's 77 communities, ICA will focus special attention on training, planning, and monitoring within selected neighborhoods that represent the geographic, economic, and ethnic diversity of the city. The sharing of documented results from these neighborhoods will serve as stimulating examples of possibility and practical action for all communities in the city.

The anticipated result will be an expansion of effective and creative community initiatives that will significantly accelerate local contributions to the success of the Chicago Climate Action Plan by 2020.

Addressing Conflict in Development: Using ICA's Technology of Participation

Jonathan Dudding

The Technology of Participation (ToP) is the name now given to the body of methods, processes and techniques that embody the approach taken by the Institute of Cultural Affairs (ICA) over the past 50 years. The approach was designed to empower local citizens to be involved in the decisions that affected their lives and has broadened to include not just the decision-making processes of communities, but also to include the state and other public authorities, companies, organisations and other entities. While ToP may not have been developed specifically as a methodology to address conflict, it is rooted in a recognition that there are differences between people, ideas, goals or values, that these differences are to be respected and accepted as part of reality and that development and change will only come about when such differences are recognised, reconciled and incorporated into the way forward. The approach uses the energy inherent in systemic conflict to drive the participants of multi-stakeholder, multi-topic conflicts toward positive solutions and working relationships.

Example 1: Villa El Salvador Industrial Park, Peru

The 288 hectare Industrial Park had all of its infrastructure installed and yet stood vacant for years due to political conflict. Meanwhile, there were hundreds of small industries operating in nearby family homes. The challenge was to form the people into industrial guilds and empower them to call for an end to the conflicts blocking the opening of the Industrial Park. In order to implement this project, the United Nations contracted the services of the ICA. This led to the formation of six industrial guilds which each made their strategic plans, and to this day maintain their separate areas in the Industrial Park. Construction and operation of a small demonstration factory making fresh cheese was the catalytic action which released the political conflict when confronted with responsible citizen organization, thereby allowing the implementation of the Industrial Park to move forward, with the assistance of the United Nations Industrial Development Organisation (UNIDO). Today the Industrial Park of Villa El Salvador houses over 1,000 industries which provide employment to over 20,000 people. (http://www.ica-peru.org/en_proyectos-urban.htm)

As the use of ToP developed and expanded, during the 1990s ICA Canada carried out an analysis of using ToP in conflict. They identified several stages of a process, now called the Phases of Conciliation [1].

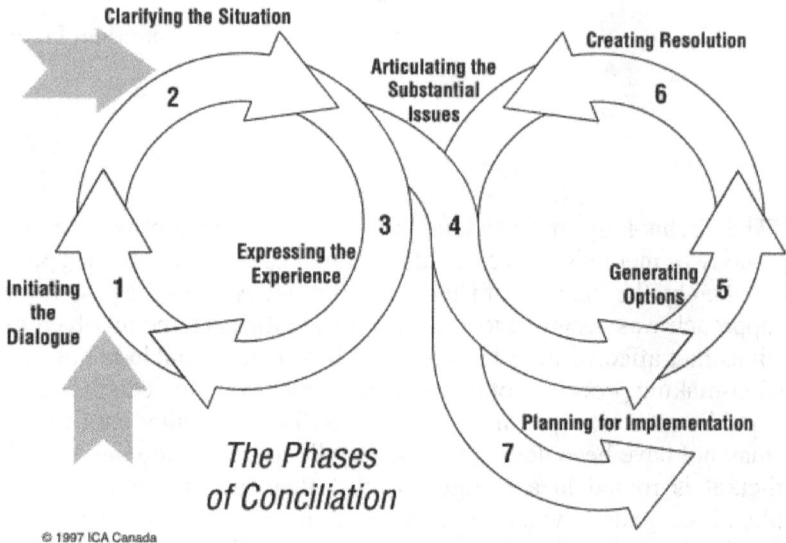

Figure 1: The Phases of Conciliation (ICA Canada, 1997)

As well as being a tool in itself, the Phases of Conciliation can also be used as a design process for addressing large and small scale conflict (see Example 2). Different ToP tools and methods (e.g. Rational and Experiential Aims, Focused Conversation, Consensus Workshop, use of Image, Participatory Strategic Planning, Contradictional Thinking/Levels of Discernment and others) can be used at each stage.

Example 2: Ontario Hydro and Wahta Mohawks First Nation, Canada

ICA Canada was engaged to facilitate negotiations over grievances related to the construction and operation of a hydro electric generating station resulting in flooding in the Wahta Mohawks First Nation in Canada. The hydro company had also routed hydro transmission lines across Mohawk territory. This mirrored decades of history of land grievances and threatened to stop the hydro project. ICA Canada was engaged to work with representatives of Hydro One and Ontario Power Generation and the community leadership of Wahta Mohawks First Nation. Wayne Nelson facilitated a team of 12 people over three years affecting 400 First Nations members and the Corporate Management of Ontario Power Generation and Hydro One.

The three year project involved designing, facilitating and documenting a process to reach a commonly agreed upon resolution of the grievances. The entire project used elements of negotiation, conflict resolution, cross cultural communication, facilitation design, process facilitation, documentation, and report writing. ToP methods were used through the project. The process resulted in a settlement that integrated the perspectives of the parties involved and was ratified by Hydro management and the community members. (http://top-facilitators.com/serendipity)

When using ToP in conflict, one "way in" is often to have people develop a shared vision - what they want to have achieved in a specific timeframe- so that any blocks or obstacles can be analysed within the context of such a vision and strategies designed to address them. The assumption is that you do not necessarily have to dig deep into the past to unearth and address deeper issues, but rather the group will be able to overcome their differences by working together towards an agreed vision or to create an alternative model which can then replace the version that is causing the difficulties (see Example 3).

Example 3: Working with Sarajevo municipalities, Bosnia and Herzegovina

In the 1990s, working in 6 municipalities in Sarajevo with World Vision under funding from UNHCR's Open Cities program, the purpose was to attract fearful minorities back to the homes they had abandoned in enclaves now dominated by another ethnic group. The process used was:

1. Train municipal authorities in basic ToP (usually about 20 people).
2. Identify local respected community leaders and train them in basic ToP (usually about 20, with as much gender and ethnic diversity as possible given that few minorities remained).
3. Bring together both groups for Participatory Strategic Planning (PSP) for their community, with a focus question that raised the need to attract back the minorities by making the community safe for them to return.
4. In the action planning phase, try to get them focused on doable things, with small amounts of funding available from United Nations High Commission for Refugees (UNHCR).
5. Post strategic planning, hold meetings to actually develop the grant proposals.

The intent was not to surface grievances or revisit pain. Those of us using the ToP methods were not trained specifically in dealing with psychological trauma, and it might have been dangerous for us to engage in that aspect of the situation, but there were many other organizations on the ground working on the psycho-social aspects of post-conflict in the region, and most of our participants already had access to that kind of care if they wanted it. Susan's theory, based on her own experience, was that when people who think they hate each other work together for a common goal, they can pull themselves out of the morass of anger and pain.

This was not easy work. There was subtle sabotage from people who wanted the UNHCR money but did not want the refugees to return. At the outset there was lack of confidence in the methods by the community leaders, who felt it might be a trick of some kind. The municipal authorities participating were fearful of giving up power to the community. And then when we got to the strategic directions and the action planning, many wanted impossible things (e.g. get the huge, abandoned, communist-style factory working again so we'll all have jobs). But the fact was that people who distrusted each other and didn't even want to sit at the same table with each other in the workshops couldn't help but get excited as the process unfolded. (Susan Fertig-Dykes, personal communication).

So what have we learnt?

As we consider the different tools and examples of ToP being used in different contexts, there are a number of insights we can draw which point both to the key contributions and limitations of ToP in conflict situations:

1. The approach is action-orientated. ToP seeks to create an environment in which people can discuss their issues and come up with a way of moving forward. As is shown in the Sarajevo example, even if some of the deeper issues remain, there is a sense that getting people to work together (and therefore to talk more with each other in the process) is a practical way of helping people move towards something they all share.
2. There is an assumption behind this that people are ready, or can be got to a point, where they are ready to use the word "we" when sitting beside other conflict parties. In cases where this is not the case, the process is unlikely to succeed unless there has been careful preparation beforehand (see Example 4).

Example 4: Working with Organisations, Malaysia

LENS International, Malaysia, has had several clients where conflict has emerged at the board level with directors not in agreement with each other in one case, and in another case, with the chairman and president not speaking to one another. In each of these cases the companies wanted us to facilitate a ToP strategic planning process with the board and senior management.

Upon learning about the conflict at the highest levels, we knew some work needed to be done prior to the planning sessions. Our decision was to request interviews with each member of these board-level groups in advance of the planning sessions. The interviews were carried out individually and notes taken and collated under themes (no names). Meetings were then scheduled with the boards and notes presented followed by a Focused Conversation ending with next steps for a successful strategic planning. The resulting meetings evolved quite differently with these two clients - in one there were tears with the president and chairman gradually talking to each other and shaking hands; in the other quite a lot of heated discussion emerged among the various members, but they also came to an understanding that they were all sharing the same vision and that in the planning, they would work out a common strategy where they knew there would be different perspectives.

To make a long story short both of the strategic planning sessions went very well subsequent to the interviews and board meetings. Additional managers attended besides the ones we interviewed and met with previously. (Ann Epps, personal communication)

3.　Often ToP practitioners use a vision-led approach (based on the thinking behind the PSP method), working with people to enable them to imagine what their future could look like, before going onto analyse the blocks and obstacles that prevent them from achieving that vision. This contrasts with other more problem-led approaches.

4.　The emphasis in ToP is on process rather than content. In other words, the focus is on enabling people to come up with their own ideas and solutions, based on their own wisdom and understanding of the situation. While this may lead to greater acceptance of ICA as an intervening agency (see Example 5) this approach may be challenged in situations where the "wisdom of the group" has been so undermined and eroded by years (even generations) of fraught existence and hatred of "the other" that the role of the facilitator has to go beyond asking questions to providing much more substantive insight and guidance both to support and help the group in their discussions and decision-making.

Example 5: Building Civil Society in Far Western Region of Nepal

ICA Nepal has been launching a project entitled "Building Civil Society through Facilitative Planning, Conflict Resolution and Peace Building Activities in three districts of Far Western region of Nepal". It has been implemented in nine village development committees of Dadeldhura, Doti and Baitadi districts. The project includes activities on training/facilitation, literacy, awareness raising, construction of environmentally sound and low cost toilets, sustainable agriculture, micro credit and human rights.

ICA carried out massive training to government staff during the conflict. The participants were trained on dealing conflict by applying facilitative approaches. They were trained on Group Facilitation Methods (GFM) and PSP so that they could tackle conflicting issues at local level. In addition, people were trained to develop conflict-sensitive plans: By using PSP, local people in remote areas were trained on developing conflict sensitive plans so that they could cope up with the threat of conflicts.

ICA Nepal involved both the conflicting parties at local level to sort out the causes and consequences of conflicts. In some cases, we invited both the parties to resolve the conflicts. Basic participatory tools such as GFM and PSP were used to handle the situation.

As we applied participatory tools and techniques in the community development work, we were never threatened by any parties. In some cases, all the NGOs were kicked out from the village as the Maoists thought they were increasing dependency at the local level, ICA in Nepal was always welcomed even by such groups as we were using facilitative tools giving due respect and credit to all the people of the community. (Tatwa Timsina, personal communication)

5.   Although ToP may be defined as a set of tools or methods, it is more than that. The combination of many years of research and experiential learning means that ToP is more of an approach, informed by and reflecting a set of values and practices that not only means careful and relevant adaptation of methods, but pays attention to all the different factors that need to be considered if a group are to feel able to participate meaningfully, including caring for the space they are in. It is this holistic approach to participation (reflected by the Rational and Experiential Aims) which helps ToP to succeed (see Example 6).

Example 6: Leadership Training in Peru

ICA Peru offers a 3-week Leadership Formation program every month to a group of 30 leaders from a small group of adjacent communities. We had a wonderful example of the effectiveness of this program in July 2010 with a group from Catahuasi District in the central sierra of Peru. This District had a long history of often violent conflict and the mayor was a dictatorial-type who would work with no one. In our program were three candidates for mayor to unseat this guy in the October elections. The three came into our program aggressively attacking each other which continued for much of the first week, which was a pretty tense time for everyone. But in the second week they began to talk to each other, and by the third week they were planning together. After our program they got together with many community members and decided that one of the three would be supported by all, and Abram was elected and is now the mayor. The demeanor has changed remarkably in the community and the people now know that they can really be in charge of their community. (Ken Hamje, personal communication)

---

6.   Using ToP enables facilitators and practitioners to bring together in one process aspects of conflict prevention, resolution and transformation, peacebuilding and community development. All too often it seems that the different areas are seen as separate disciplines, each with their own proponents and methodologies. ToP cuts through this by its stance of "life is as it is" and its focus on process, taking individuals, groups and communities on a journey and able to support them all along the way (see Example 7)

106 • Changing Lives, Changing Societies
ICA's Experience in Nepal and in the World

Example 7: Participatory Project Prioritization, Afghanistan

In 2010 ToP practitioner Alisa Oyler worked in Afghanistan with the International Non-Government Organisation Mercy Corps to develop a standard community mobilization methodology as part of the multi-province Community Development Program. This was largely intended to mitigate possible conflict in communities going through a project selection process. In addition to some other elements, the mobilization included a Participatory Project Prioritization Process (P4M) Meeting format that blends a little ToP (a variation of a vision workshop using pictures instead of words) with some Participatory Rural Appraisal (PRA) methods. As a participant, Haji Safar from Kaldar district (Balkh Province) said "*asking local people for identifying their problems, is a really impressive approach to motivate and empower us to stand on our feet and to really contribute to stabilization and sustain local resources*". (Alisa Oyler, personal communication)

Looking at the future for ToP being used in conflict, there are two main directions that seem to be emerging:

1.   Compartmentalisation of disciplines and thinking has led to ToP being categorised too narrowly under the community or organisational development banner. This does justice neither to the complexity and inter-connectedness of the issues being addressed, nor to the breadth and depth of what ToP can contribute to groups in conflict. So one direction is to work to break down some of these false differentiations and raise the profile of ToP as a methodology which has something to offer those focusing on conflict, and to encourage greater cross-fertilisation of all approaches and methods.

2.   There is now a whole range of approaches and methods which have been tried and tested in conflict. There is real value in considering how the different methods and approaches can be combined (even integrated) to provide the most powerful approach that we can to work with people who are suffering from being in a conflict and who want to move on. This is very much the approach taken by the Kumi project[1] which started in Israel and Palestine, but which is now beginning to explore how the method and approach developed can be applied in other conflicts and other places. Kumi brought together ToP practitioners and experts in identity based conflict and in conflict analysis. Out of this has emerged a process which is arguably more powerful than any of our approaches could have delivered on their own, but which at the same time, reflects the values and principles

1 See www.ica-uk.org.uk/research for further details on the Kumi project

of all of them. Such combination and integration of ToP with other methods is already happening in less conflicted scenarios but with equal effect.

Acknowledgements

With thanks to the many ToP practitioners from around the world who shared their experiences and helped my thinking: Rosemary

Cairns, Clive Downs, Marilyn Doyle, Ann Epps, Susan Fertig-Dykes, Gerald Gomani, Ken Hamje, Ann Lukens, Alisa Oyler, Bill Staples, Tatwa Timsina. Not all of their examples have been included here, but I hope their lessons and insights have been sufficiently reflected.

References

1. ICA Canada (2007), *Facilitating Conciliation* Trainers and Participants' manuals

2. These case studies and others demonstrating and recording the use of ToP in conflict and in many other situations can be found at http://top-facilitators.com/serendipity and/or http://site.top-facilitators.com

Decentralised Transformative Approaches To HIV and AIDS - An Experience of ICA-Nepal

Janet Sanders, Tatwa P. Timsina, Juju Raj Tuladhar and Richard Sims

ICA –Nepal conducted a year long programme on Decentralized Transformative Approaches to HIV/AIDS with the support of UNDP together with UNAIDS and Nepal Center for AIDS and STD Control of the Government of Nepal. Representatives from various government departments, I/NGO, media persons, private sectors, civil society and vulnerable groups for HIV/AIDS were the major target groups of this programme. This project was continued in many other districts through POLICY Project, Local Development Training Academy and Ministry of Local Development in which ICA Nepal also actively participated as facilitating organization.

Global Scenario

HIV/AIDS is a global pandemic problem. Every day, about 14000 people are infected with HIV. It is estimated that more than 5 million people catch HIV each year. By 2005 about 25 million have died from HIV/AIDS and 40 million are believed to be living with HIV/AIDS around the world. As no total effective medicines have been developed, prevention is the only hope for controlling this pandemic in the world. Almost 30 years after the first case of HIV was reported, it has spread around the globe to become the biggest pandemic ever. In 2009, 1.8 million people died from AIDS-related illnesses - nearly one-fifth lower than the 2.1 million people who died in 2004.

Facts of HIV and AIDS in Nepal (1988 – 2009)

- The first AIDS case in Nepal was reported in 1988.
- As of 2009, national estimates indicate that about 63,528 adults and children are affected with HIV.
- The epidemic scenario is now described as "mixed": 54% of the infections are among the relatively low risk male and female population.

- In 2009, about 31% of reported HIV cases comprised of women aged 15-49 years.
- Children (0-14) represented 6.5% of the reported infections.
- Distribution of reported infections: IDUs: 16%, FSWs: 5%, MSM: 1%, clients of FSW: 44%, housewives: 26%.
- Young people aged 15-27 are very vulnerable to contracting HIV as 72% of females and 56% of males have yet to acquire comprehensive HIV knowledge.
- Among Nepali migrants traveling to Indian cities, approximately 16% engage in high risk sexual behaviour or visit sex workers.

The Causes of HIV/AIDS in Nepal

The HIV virus is transmitted mainly through unsafe sex and blood transfusions. The epidemic in Nepal is driven by IDUs (intravenous drug users), migrants, sex workers and their clients, and MSM (men sex men), FSW (Female sex workers), and street children. Results from the 2007 Integrated Bio-Behavioral Surveillance Study (IBBS) among IDUs in Kathmandu, Pokhara, and East and West Terai indicate that the highest prevalence rates have been found among urban IDUs, 6.8 percent to 34.7 percent of whom are HIV-positive.

Nepal's 1.5 million to 2 million labor migrants account for the majority of Nepal's HIV-positive population. In one subgroup, 2.8 percent of migrants returning from Mumbai, India, were infected with HIV. As of 2007, HIV prevalence among FSWs and their clients was less than 2 percent and 1 percent respectively, and 3.3 percent among urban-based MSM. HIV and AIDS case reporting by the NCASC reports HIV infections to be more common among men than women, as well as in urban areas and the far western region of the country, where migrant labor is more common.

Street children are also one of the most vulnerable groups. The UNICEF report, "Increasing Vulnerability of Children in Nepal", estimates the number of children orphaned by HIV/AIDS to be more than 13,000. The national estimate of children 0 to 14 years of age infected by HIV is 2,500 (2007). According to Nepal's 2007 United Nations General Assembly Special Session (UNGASS) report, labor migrants make up 41 percent of the total known HIV infections in the country, followed by clients of sex workers (15.5 percent) and IDUs (10.2 percent).

The Nepal Project in Brief

The *Decentralised Transformative Approaches to HIV-AIDS* programme series, launched in Nepal Fall 2002, **leverages the strength of Nepal's established decentralized governance system** and builds upon the growing political will among Nepal's leaders to address HIV/AIDS as a development issue of nationwide importance.

Before the project, there were already many building blocks in place to address the epidemic, including inventive responses at the local level. However, there was a lack of functional coordination and networking among government and non-government organizations. District Development Committees (DDCs) were beginning to pick up the mandate of response to the epidemic through the devolution of health powers. The large number of NGOs and INGOs involved in the response to HIV-AIDS in Nepal were slowly being integrated with, government policy and agencies.

ICA Nepal has been working on leadership curriculum since 2001 when it became the National coordinator for the Pilot program of Leadership for Results work in Nepal. The program was a partnership between HIV/AIDS work headed up by Monica Sharma and Decentralization headed by Rob Work. Jan Sanders was the International consultant and Tatwa P. Timsina the National coordinator. Its uniqueness was to focus on both the understanding of responsible action in face of the epidemic and a focus on the individual ability to increase capacity to affect change through developing their self and social awareness.

Nepal was chosen for this District Decentralized Transformative Approach because of its past history of decentralisation, the level of the epidemic, the stigma attached to and isolation imposed upon those living with HIV-AIDS, and the current critical demand for effective multi-sector intervention.

For the project, three 10-day capacity development modules focused on leadership development and dynamic planning were conducted between June 2002 and July 2003, facilitated by leadership expert Janet Sanders and co-facilitators Tatwa Timsina and Narayan Pradhan. The UN Thematic Group on HIV-AIDS provided national linkages and advice for the approach. The events were hosted in Morang and Sunsari District selected to be 'teaching districts' because of the level of HIV-AIDS activities already occurring. Existing activities could be scaled out to other parts of the districts and across other regions and these districts could enter into creative dialogue with national actors on policy and programme initiative. This approach builds on the courageous initiatives already in place to combat HIV-AIDS, strengthens district leadership and participatory multi-sector planning, seeks to clarify the district government response and creates nationwide networks to effectively respond to HIV-AIDS.

Twenty-two outstanding contributors to Nepal's district-level HIV-AIDS response were recruited as resource persons for the seminars and were trained to continue facilitating the development of transformative HIV-AIDS leadership in Nepal – leadership that envisions possibilities and creates opportunities previously unimagined, and brings voice to those previously unheard.

Over 200 participants, from NGOs, CBOs, women's groups, youth groups, PLWHA, media, national and sub-national government (District Development Committees) were guided through task-focused individual and team work towards developing an informed, empowered and committed leadership base at the District Level that engages all available socio-political resources in order to achieve nationwide results in the reversal of the epidemic.

The approach worked through the Ministry of Health and the National Centre for AIDS and STD Control (NCASC), and the United Nations Country Team on HIV-AIDS. The National Strategic Plan (2003) of GoN/ Nepal Ministry of Health, through the National Centre for AIDS and STD Control and the National AIDS Council, calls for the decentralisation of health and the participation of multi-sectors in planning and implementation.

Morang and Sunsari Districts in Eastern Nepal were selected as the two 'labs' for the approach. For national coverage and scaling up opportunities participants came from one district in each region. These included Dadeldhura, Banke, Parbat, Baktapur, and Saptari.

Measurable outcomes of the Nepal project include:

- **113 district-level leaders from all 5 regions of Nepal** with enhanced and diversified HIV-AIDS leadership competency, actively engaged in actions within the context of a nation-wide response;

- **22 trained Nepali facilitators** prepared to promulgate the Leadership for Results capacity development approach at district and regional levels;

- **A district AIDS plan in both Morang and Sunsari districts,** harmonized with and key national response objectives and beginning to be implemented;

- Morang and Sunsari districts each building a **results-oriented network** of 90 people committed to work together to respond to HIV-AIDS;

- **Linkages created with national level** response of the National Centre for STD and AIDS, the Ministry of Health, and UN system.

- ICA Nepal and the Nepal facilitators continue to be active in HIV/AIDS programs. The planning processes were incorporated into development planning at the district level.

FOUR KEY COMPONENTS:

There are four key, linked components to the DTAHA:

A. Transformation Leadership Seminars and Facilitator Training
B. Dynamic Planning and Implementation
C. Formation of District Networks
D. Practice of Commitment

FRAMEWORK

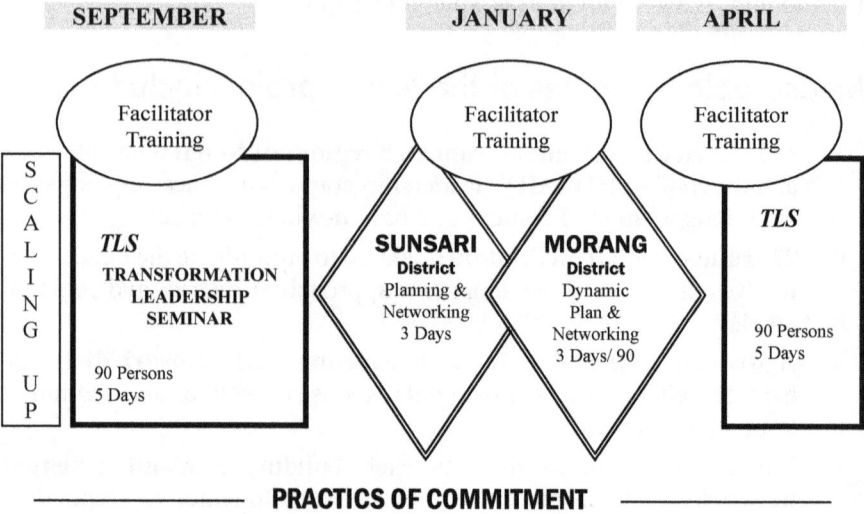

A. Transformation Leadership Seminars

> Finding the centre of strength within
> ourselves is in the long run the best
> contribution we can make to our fellow
> humans.
>
> *R. Walsh*

The transformation leadership seminars build upon the conclusions of the UNGASS conference calling for the courage to take risks, innovate, and expand interventions on a scale never before achieved in order to reverse the spread of HIV-AIDS. This challenge requires leaders to look deep within themselves for inner strengths and resources and also to understand all of the underlying factors and far reaching consequences of the epidemic, thus addressing the true depth and breadth of the issue. Through three leadership seminars, DTAHA provided the opportunity for a cross-section of participants from seven districts to focus on individual introspection, acquire skills for planning and action, and build a trusting, cross-sectoral network for on-going dialogue, collaboration and action. Seminars included time for work both on **"Inner Leadership"** and **"Leadership in Action"**.

Seminar Frameworks

The Transformation Leadership Seminars were informed by the following frameworks:

- The **Emotional Intelligence Framework** was used for participants to examine their own strengths, resources, values, beliefs, and self-confidence. They formed a vision of themselves as leaders and focus on developing the social, self-management and relationship skills to acquire a new leadership style. Through introspection and reflection they empowered themselves to realize their full potential as change agents of human development. Practices were incorporated from Brian Stanfield's book The Courage to Lead and Dr. Jean Houston's work on Social Artistry.

- Ken Wilber's **Four-Quadrant Framework** allowed the participants to develop a **complex holistic understanding** of the HIV-AIDS epidemic. The holistic framework allowed leaders to ask the right questions, see the bigger picture and work towards sustainable results. The model let the leaders see the links between individual and group attitudes, norms and values, and the consequent behaviour and actions.

- **Strategic Reflection and Planning Process**: helped leaders to develop the capacity to facilitate large group planning processes using ToP (Technology of Participation) and the Appreciative Inquiry methods. The Workshop and Discussion Methods were also utilized in the planning processes. Systems thinking, the role of the leaders in organizations, and the Principles for 'Action at Scale' were included in the agenda.

- The leaders built a shared leadership network of District actors, based on horizontal links of individual initiative and collaboration following the **Lickert** model. They developed their **"external leadership"** through learning skills in the areas of leading groups in conversations, workshops and dynamic planning.

- **HIV and Me** provided the framework for exploring individual responses to the virus, participants' sexual practices, depth understanding on the causes of the spread, empathy for those living with the virus and their families, and innovative responses.

Innovative Techniques and Tools

- Brainstorming and Mind Mapping
- Varieties of Group Discussion Methods
- Mental Rehearsal/Applied Imagination
- Self-Awareness Practices
- Social and Learning Styles
- Four Levels of Social Artist's Awareness.

B. Dynamic Planning and Implementation

The District Development Committees of Morang and Sunsari each sponsored a Dynamic Planning Process. The dynamic planning and implementation process builds upon current strengths and assets, allows participants to envision a possible future, analyses the complex nature of the factors which fuel the spread of the virus and to work in partnership to design and implement a multi-sectoral response. Throughout the process the 90 participants from a cross section of the district challenge themselves expanding their commitment and leadership capacities. Half of the group attending the planning were from the Transformation Leadership Seminars and the additional participants were from district government, community organisation and the media.

Principles for good governance were incorporated, including accountability, transparency, and responsiveness. The results are a district strategic framework for HIV-AIDS and a network with a mandate for sustained coordinated action. In the planning the participants interacted with those from the National Centre for AIDS and STD Control (NCASC) and the National HIV-AIDS Strategy. The Plan incorporated initiatives at the individual, organisational and institutional levels.

Following the three-day session an advisory committee was set-up to review the plan and put it into a **logical framework** for submission to the District Development Committee on AIDS. The advisory taskforce presented the completed plan to a one-day gathering of the HIV-AIDS district network for review and comment. A final draft was presented to each District Development Committee for AIDS who has shared it with the Ministry of Health, NCASC and the National Planning Commission for their review and acceptance. The DDC pledged 15% of the financing of the plan and committed to securing finances for the remaining components.

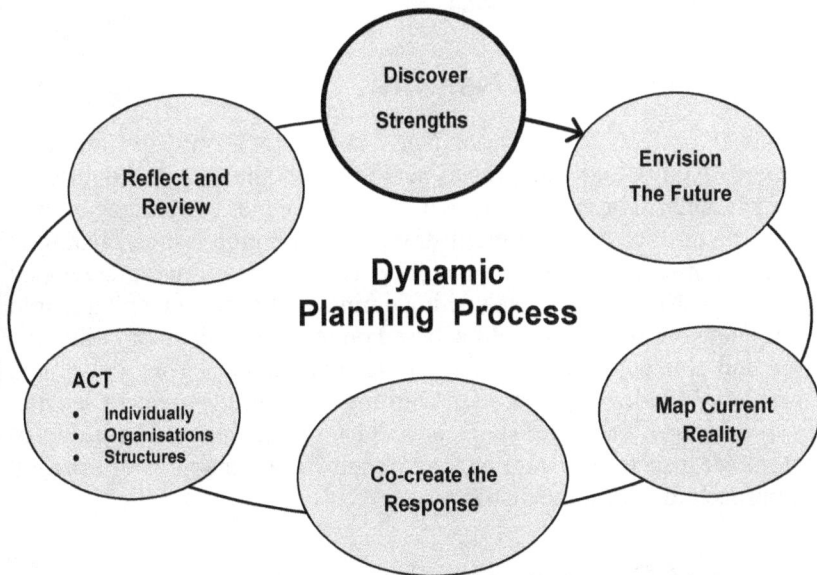

The Dynamic planning process builds both upon the pioneering work of the Institute of Cultural Affairs work in 'Technology of Participation and the Appreciative Inquiry Methods.

Key elements of success in the Dynamic Planning Process

- Sponsorship by key government stakeholder (s).
- Leaders trained through Transformation Leadership Seminars.
- Breadth and depth of recruitment across sectors, geography, ages. Movement beyond the usual stakeholders.
- Beyond recruitment, all stakeholders played prominently in decision-making including people living with HIV-AIDS and women.
- Opportunities for small group dialogue to allow all voices to be heard, to engage thoughts, to share own accomplishments and eventually, to develop group voice.
- Creation of opportunities for individual commitments and coordination of responses.
- Provision of adequate time for the planning process.
- Modeling of new style of leadership through planning process.
- Incorporation in the Dynamic Plan of strategies that would be implemented by individuals, organisation and the district government.
- It is expected that the approach has positively influenced in decreasing the rate of HIV cases in Nepal.

C. Formation of District Networks

In the Nepal project, two District Networks were formulated allowing government, NGOs and the private sector to continue to build bridges toward each other. These networks will also be vehicles to continue to look at the 'big picture' of AIDS in the district, flag emerging issues, champion emerging responses and hold accountability. These networks were developed during the Transformational Leadership Seminars. The leaders built a shared leadership network of District actors, based on horizontal links of individual initiative and collaboration following the **Lickert** model. They developed their **"external leadership"** through learning skills in the areas of leading groups in conversations, workshops and dynamic planning. The group of facilitators has also formed into a national network to enable an up scaling of the approach to additional districts.

D. Practice of Commitment

In order to encourage leaders to practice new skills and perspectives through action learning, and to empower team collaboration on planning processes, participants were asked to develop individual **Practices of Commitment**.

These were each leader's personal commitment and contribution to an extraordinary response to HIV-AIDS. Each commitment was to stretch the individual's leadership capacities and initiate actions towards the four HIV-AIDS strategies.

Decentralisation

A major facet of this redefinition is informed by the concept of decentralisation, a challenging and complex process that promises to be a mechanism for improved democratic governance and sustainable human development. (Overview of Decentralisation Worldwide: A Stepping Stone to Improved Governance and Human Development).

Some of the opportunities included in decentralisation are:
- increased participation of individuals in assuming responsibility for initiatives
- increased efficiency in determining the real situation and service demands
- flexibility in the face of changing circumstances
- capacity to tailor situations to local needs
- wide diversity of innovations that can feed into policy and programming responses
- promotion of a knowing and acceptance of various cultures within a geographic setting
- the ability to take successful local initiatives and scale them out to other communities
- the ability to effectively tap local resources
- the innovations that result from decentralisation often benefit local governments through increased global communications and international and regional networking.

Role of National, District and Local Levels

Decentralisation always involves changes of relationships between and among different societal actors, social sectors and geographic areas. In the DTAHA, the main area of activity or entry point was the district level. The **district level's key strength** is its **links** to both the **local and the national** levels.

The DTA: Nepal created geographical networks with a coordinated plan. The uniqueness of the approach is found in the principles of decentralisation. This project is a complex weave of the national, district and local actors.

A shift in perspective would begin to see the three levels on a horizontal plane, each with its own unique role.

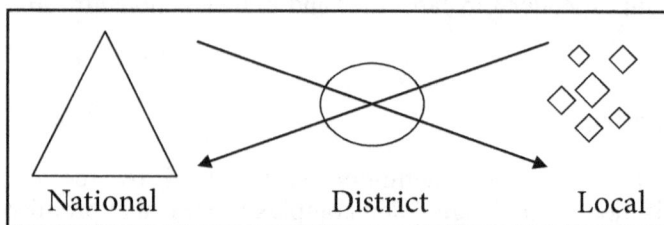

National   District   Local

Local groups, implementing real activities with concrete results, leverage their efforts and resources through coordination in the district network. The silo walls between NGOs (non-governmental organizations) and CBOs (community based organizations) programmes have the potential to disappear in the **district network** with initiatives becoming mutually reinforcing. The shared leadership (decentralisation) at the district level allows for customizing the national programmes and resources to meet the needs of the specific issues in their geography.

At the **national level**, policy, funding priorities and public advocacy are informed by the real situation through input from the district networks. With superior training, the district/local actors become the experts. Leadership comes from the field.

Transformation of the Individual to increase capacity to affect change

In redefining responsibility for action, individual action is recognized as an essential component for change. In order for individuals to be capable of and empowered to affect change, attention must be given to individual leadership development.

Part of the DTAHA was helping individuals to develop some of the leadership skills necessary to affect change. More important than the skills development, the DTAHA seminars focus a great deal on interior development, recognizing that without interior development, healthy exterior development cannot be sustained. The frameworks used, provided participants with the opportunities to build upon the capacity that already exists within each of them and within the culture as a whole. This approach was not about facilitators "teaching" participants how to be leaders. Rather, it was providing opportunities for individuals to become aware of and strengthen their own internal leadership capabilities.

Transformation of the individual helps participants to increase their capacity to affect change. This capacity building also means that these individuals can provide support to others in their community comparable to that which they received from the DTAHA team. This ripple effect will facilitate continuity of the work being done.

Conclusion

A. Leadership for Results Frameworks

"The world, which we have made as a result of the level of thinking we have done thus far, creates problems that we cannot solve at the same level at which we created them". Albert Einstein

FIVE FRAMEWORKS

The following five conceptual models form the basic underlying structure for Nepal's Leadership for Results Programme:

1. Transformational Leadership Competencies
2. Likert's Levels of Organizational Development
3. Emotional Intelligence Framework
4. Four- Quadrant Framework –Holistic Thinking
5. Dynamic Planning Process with Technology of Participation

1. Transformational Leadership Competencies

Leadership is a conscious process, starting with clarity about one's own personal goals and how these fit with the mission of the organization and with the strategy. Leadership requires that a person be highly self aware, able to manage one's self in stressful and complex environments, able to 'read' other people, empathize with their needs and lead others to get the job done. Leaders need to know what inhibits effective individual and team performance and how to address these blocks. In other words, leadership requires a deep understanding of how social systems – and the people in them—must work together to achieve complex and challenging goals.

What separates leaders from followers is the language they use, the environment they create, the meaning they make of the current situation, and how they communicate that to others. Therefore, when faced with challenging, perhaps even overwhelming situations, such as the HIV/

AIDS pandemic for example, effective leaders draw upon tools that help them perceive the situation differently and enable others to respond based on the opening they create. Awareness of these kinds of competencies and distinctions are critical for leaders in today's demanding workplace, especially so for leaders that work in the response to HIV/AIDS, in which no magic bullet formula or road map yet exists.

Transformational Leadership:

Generating Shared Commitments towards a Shared Future

- Leadership is Being, Speaking, Listening, and Acting in a way that enables a community to effectively meet the challenges it faces

- Transformation occurs when you recognize, acknowledge, and give up an automatic "way of being" in favour of making something new possible

- The certainty with which a leader acts comes from their commitments

- Transformational Leadership is centered in self; expressed in community

- To build successful coalitions, listen for what goals there are in common, instead of attending to what's different.

Self-Directed Leadership: A Journey of Discovery

One cannot be mandated to learn or develop their leadership capabilities, they must be self-directed if the process is to really work. This type of leadership development means getting a clear image of the type of leaders you want to be and an accurate picture of your real self. Change often means shifting habits, which have been learned early in life. Developing new capabilities takes time and practice until the behaviour becomes automatic.

Primal Leadership: Realizing the Power of Emotional Intelligence, by *Daniel Goleman, Richard Boyatzis and Annie McKee*

The Courage to Lead by *Brian Stanfield* and The Possible Human by *Dr. Jean Houston* for exercises used in the five discoveries.

Kamananda, a newly appointed community health worker is one example. He was a shy person. After the first training session, he has initiated and conducted 10 training sessions. He was asked, "What image of yourself did you have when you first came to the TLS?" He replied that he was afraid to initiate things because he might be called a foolish person. "Now what kind of image do you have of yourself? He said, "I have gained confidence. I am not afraid to take the lead now. I began by giving presentations during the training and I went back to my community and began practicing with family members who needed to hear the causes of HIV-AIDS."

2. Likert's Levels of Organization Development

The Rensis Likert Scale, a model of organizational development, describes how organizations and institutions evolve through different stages, and how they—through strategic and conscious effort—can change their focus, goals and operating structures to become more self-aware, principled and effective. Every level that is achieved incorporates the strengths and lessons learned of the previous levels, but transcends their limitations to operate at a more integrated and effective level.

3. Emotional Intelligence

"Great leaders move us. They ignite our passion and inspire the best in us."

Primal Leadership: Realizing the Power of Emotional Intelligence, *Daniel Goleman, Richard Boyatzis and Annie McKee, Harvard Business School Press, March 2002.*

Emotional intelligence describes abilities distinct from, but complementary to, academic intelligence or the purely cognitive capacities measured by IQ, enabling leaders to better deal with their own internal responses and state of mind, as well as how they deal with others. Specifically, emotionally intelligent leaders are able to do the following effectively:

- Act in ways that leave the people around them (partners, team members, employees, community members, etc) feeling stronger and more capable;
- Manage themselves effectively under stress and/or when dealing with ambiguous circumstances; remain calm and stay focused; and
- Stay intensely in touch with what the people they lead are thinking and feeling, to motivate and energize them.

4. Holistic Thinking: The Four-Quadrant Framework Aligning Values and Action

The Four-Quadrant Framework helps facilitate awareness of the interaction between different domains of experience: Attitudes and actions, individual and group, social systems and societal structures. It deepens understanding of the HIV/AIDS epidemic by demonstrating the links between the individual and group attitudes or norms and consequent actions by individuals and groups. In planning for an expanded, extraordinary response, at individual, community and societal levels, it is important that we understand and employ these dynamics in our strategies to produce the desired results. The Four-Quadrant Framework lends itself very well to mapping exercises that graphically plot current reality from the perspective of 4 distinct domains:

Mapping current reality allows us to put the HIV/AIDS epidemic in its social, economic and cultural context within a given country or locale. Mapping exercises look specifically at situations that may be relevant to HIV, the factors that favor the acceleration or impede its spread, and the factors that favor or impede achieving the best possible quality of life for those living with HIV/AIDS or for their families, friends and communities. For example, it is vital that we consider societal and individual values and actions in our strategic planning. The strategic planning process can be both a technical exercises and a truly effective, empowering and transformative process that aligns values and actions.

Practice of Commitment Reflection using Wilbur Framework

Context: Often when we debrief a project we focus on the external outcomes: What happened? What did we accomplish? Who was involved? In our debriefing we wanted to look at the internal outcomes both on the individual level and to those who participated (collective). These questions are for suggestions—others might be added or subtracted.

Talking Circles

The facilitator from her work in Indigenous cultures shared with the seminar participants the 'talking circle' as a way to reflect at a deeper level on the topic of HIV/AIDS as it relates to your experience. The process creates 'safe space', to enable participants to talk about their lives openly and completely. It is intended to be simple, yet profound. It is a time of listening deeply to oneself and each other from a place of understanding not from judgment or trying to 'fix them'. It provides a slower pace for reflection and shared understanding.

An object such as stone or stick is used to designate the speaker. The person holding the object speaks and the other members of the circle listen. When the speaker finishes, the object is passed to the next person in the circle. This process continues until all members of the circle have spoken. No one is to interrupt the words of the speaker. It is possible to speak more than once by having more than one round in your group. Each person is given the opportunity to "speak from the heart". All content is confidential and not to be shared outside the circle unless permission is given by the speaker.

Sample of Participant Learning Statements

- I realized that if individually we all do something on HIV/AIDS, then together we could reach our goal. This practice raised my own sense of responsibility.
- We can use the new techniques to reach less engaged stakeholders.
- My learning was in self-confidence, optimism and creativity.
- Internal result was self-awareness, positive thinking; external result was initiation of group work, decision to make VDC network and share information about HIV/AIDS.
- I learned that most people do not know about HIV/AIDS, and I want to change that.
- It is much more effective to work in coordination with other organizations.
- I saw people change their attitudes about HIV/AIDS.
- I learned that to control the epidemic, we have to focus on simple things like using razor blade to shave men's beard. 95% of men were using a common knife to shave beard and it is now decreased through our awareness efforts.
- It is essential that we network with those organizations that are working in my area.
- I realized that we should change our traditional concepts about HIV/AIDS.
- Mostly the HIV/AIDS programs are conducted in the 5-star hotels of Kathmandu city. It will be more effective to conduct those programs in other areas of Nepal as well.

PELP in the Context of Earthquake and Tsunami at Bio Region

Isabel de la Maza U

On February 27, 2010, Chile suffered an 8.8° (Richter) earthquake and a terrible Tsunami. ICA-Chile had to commit supporting the victims of this tremendous natural disaster. ICA-Japan contacted ICA-Chile and they offered their help in money and experience in such a terrible emergency. For us, this was a great possibility to help our Southern fellow citizens in disgrace. ICA- Japan collaborated enormously helping us after this catastrophe. Their resources came through Japan's Platform (this is an entity that receives funding from the Japanese Government, Japanese Enterprises, and in general from Japanese citizens). We are deeply grateful to the Japanese Platform and to ICA-Japan for their uninterested collaboration and commitment.

We worked with ICA-Japan on several Analysis Workshops in order to analyze the situation the victims had suffered and preparing action plans with them so as to look for the necessary formulae that would help them overcome to the best of their possibilities the disaster they had to live.

Thanks to the donations in money we received from Japan, we were able (at the beginning) to deliver food, tents, building materials, stoves, blankets, and waterproof cloaks for the rain. Later on, thanks again to ICA-Japan we were able to deliver stoves for the near by winter time, toilet paper, disposable diapers, warm clothes, building materials in order to secure and isolate their homes, diving equipment and a machine to remove the debris. Thirdly, Japan's donations made us able to buy boat engines for the fishing boats that had already been repaired so that the inhabitants of these places - mostly fishermen - could restart their usual activities and get the necessary income to survive.

We had the intention to support emotionally these victims of the earthquake, so we planned a support program through workshops, using ICA's Technology of Participation. We received the enthusiastic collaboration of men and women volunteers in each of the communities. Besides, in Concepción we had the remarkable collaboration of volunteers from our 2009 PELP that had taken place there, led by Marcelo Machuca, Professional Psychologist, who works at the Child Rehabilitation Institute in Concepción. During 2009, he was the coordinator of PELP Program there. Thanks to Marcelo's help we were able to localize all the participants in that PELP through Facebook and with the data base we had from the former year. Once we found out that all of them were fine, we located the villages that had the worst part during the earthquake and Tsunami. Thus we arrived to Caleta de Tumbes, Talcahuano and Penco, and then we moved on to other very vulnerable places, arriving finally to Arauco.

While being in Concepción, and before contacting the volunteers and 2009 PELP participants, I had a meeting at the Child Rehabilitation Institute with its Executive Director, Dr. Violeta Hinojosa. She told me that after the earthquake, they started to work repairing the Institute's building and other premises, even though they hadn't been seriously damaged, so as to function appropriately. Later they worked on the emotional field supporting the team of professionals that worked at the Institute, because, naturally they were really moved by this disaster. Once they finished this part, patients started flowing in, speaking about all the terrible experiences they'd suffered. Some of them had very moving stories to tell. For example, a young 22 years old paraplegic woman (she uses an electric wheel chair) that suffered the strength of the Tsunami at her home. She and her children were saved thanks to the children's father, who climbed to the roof of their house with all of them. Then they moved to an Emergency Refuge with a lot of difficulties for there was no space for the wheel chair nor an appropriate bathroom for this woman's disabilities.

Even though the Child Rehabilitation Institute started functioning almost normally, they had a big traffic problem to enable patients and professionals to get there, because the bridge that connects San Pedro de la Paz and Concepción was severely damaged. So, our Telethon volunteers and young participants in our PELP, dedicated themselves to support patients and their families for a year, in order that they would reach the premises at the Institute.

As a result of this experience we can conclude that it is necessary to have a Program that connects people and that allows to establish help nets, so that these people know each other and can communicate amongst them as quickly as possible. PELP Program worked on 2009 to achieve this, thus on 2010 they could react appropriately, facing this catastrophe. Their capacity to organize, to work in teams and the strength of a closely united group and an efficient leadership proved themselves, facing a real emergency. All this happened thanks to the work we had previously developed in PELP and it was an example of support and youngsters' solidarity. This demonstrates the enormous impact and personal change that happens in the spirit of young people after they've had an experience with PELP Program.

Some PELP Facilitators and Trainers inputs.

Eduard Christensen (ICA – Chile Trainer and Facilitator)

Working with youngsters with differently able and with students, created an environment of nearness. They felt comfortable sharing habits and interests. There was an environment of mutual trust that helped them to share dreams and experiences.

Thus, they got to know each other, to talk amongst them about their achievements and their feelings establishing a positive human motivation.

This PELP Program tries to achieve a group dialogue and it is a great example, a demonstration methodology. Conversations that broaden the horizons of the young participants - men and women - who had never seen each other and that little by little all dared to practice, following the examples of the exercises we prepared for them in different workshops led by experienced facilitators. They repeated these exercises at home, and they were motivated to practice them because they were entertaining and new. The idea is to communicate, to be able to get out of one's self, to open up, to express what their senses told them: what they saw, heard and touched. That's the way they experienced their peers' feeling and answers…they were listened to and so they could express their own feelings, their sorrow and joy, their emotions, their memories, and thus they could continue in a deeper dialogue about important and significant events.

We have seen how stimulant this is in order to achieve an intercourse with their environment. They naturally achieved a communication process and we are all part of it, so we are very pleased with the positive results of these PELPs.

Isabel Rodríguez (ICA – Chile Trainer and Facilitator)

In the PELPs I've participated during these years, I've been able to observe a huge change in the lives of the youngsters we worked with. When they first came, they didn't know what to expect. They only knew that this was a Program where they would learn to work in groups and better their self-esteem.

Nevertheless, they couldn't even imagine the changes they would have due to this Program. During the meetings they started learning how to relate with their peers, to "infect" themselves with the joy, the good feelings and also to learn to listen to others with respect. They learned to express their opinions fearlessly. They shared their dreams, sorrows, their happiness and they learned how to support each other.

By the end of the Program they were able to plan and manage new projects and act accordingly. Starting with the first PELP, their friendship flourished until today. They now have a sort of net to work amongst them.

The young boys and girls gained their independence from their families for they want to be the main actors of their own lives and face the challenges the future has in store for them. Some of them were able to discover what they wanted to do for the rest of their lives.

These youngsters are searching to be totally included into the general society, through their work. They realize that we are all born with different talents/abilities, that need to be developed broad-mindedly and genuinely accepting them.

Yelmo Durán Kreither (Facilitator and "in love" with the art of facilitating groups)

My experience in PELPs is the *wonder* of sharing, learning, understanding that "it is possible". To loose the limits we have in our minds; to find the creator that inhabits our bodies; to coordinate and challenge ourselves; the wonder of knowing that the "magic" is in each and everyone of us.

The *grace* of finding human beings that are very human, to meet others and build friendships, to accept an invitation, a challenge. The grace to dare, to grow in our abilities, to practice and be persistent, to listen and observe, to understand and accept and just to keep adding up and stepping forward.

Nigel Blackburn (ToP Methods Trainer and Facilitator).

When we started thinking in PELP, we wanted to deliver the Methodology of the Technology of Participation (ToP), created by the Institute of Cultural Affairs (ICA), to some of the former patients of the Child Rehabilitation Institute, better known as the Telethon. We thought that these communication tools would be very useful to them in order to better the quality of their personal lives, their families, society and work.

At the beginning of the course we soon realized that we had opened Pandora's Box. What was really happening during the first PELP was by far more powerful than what we had expected. We noticed that applying the ToP Methodology to the course, besides its contents, the participants started showing other parts of their personality. You could see them gaining confidence in themselves and certainty in their way of acting, throwing themselves into doing things they had never imagined they could do, like leading a group of 35 people in a Consensus Workshop; prepare and lead conversations in big and small groups and doing it successfully, etc…

When we saw all this happening, we started changing each step of the Program, including in it some self development issues so our participants could reach more ambitious goals. These goals would have challenged a group of not physically challenged people. We realized that we were designing - as we walked on - something very powerful for these participants.

The values that emerged in PELPs reflect clearly the values of ICA's Methodology of Participation.

- Participation based in genuine inclusion of all participants.
- Participation based essentially in a deep respect for other people and their ideas.
- Participation that leaves no one out.
- Participation that leads to concrete activities and visible results.
- Participation that creates new bonds of friendship and mutual support.

The first PELPS were carried out in the Kinesiology room at the Institute. Each week the team would place itself in one corner of the room in order to create the space we needed. Just across this room, separated by a small garden, was the place where they took care of patients that had been recently operated on, with their full nursing equipment. These Nurses had already met many of our PELP participants, because they'd had to take care of them at some previous occasion. They kept observing us week after week, until one day, during the third PELP one of the Nurses approached me and said:... "I have no idea what you do with these youngsters during this Program, but when they finish it, they walk differently".

I was speechless. She had summarized in two words the deep power of PELP: empower youngsters to walk differently through their lives.

Implications of the Technology of Participation (ToP) Approach in Learning and Research in Bangladesh

Mohammad Azizur Rahman and Md. Mohsin Ali

Teaching and research are integral parts of higher education and human development. Along with the technological development and socioeconomic transformation of the post-world War II, various methods and techniques have been developed over the years to promote quality teaching and research at colleges and universities. Despite overwhelming advancement in science and technology, teachers and researchers still face challenges to ensure student participation for active learning and investigating human subjects. The Technology of Participation (ToP) developed by the Institute of Cultural Affairs (ICA) can in this regard contribute to addressing the challenges. The ToP has meanwhile been internationally recognized and applied as a tool for proven training, facilitation, community empowerment, and organizational transformation. Available literature suggests that the ToP has been practiced in pre-schools, high schools, and adult education training. However, there is hardly any literature on the use of the ToP in university teaching and research. Based on a review of the secondary literature, our personal teaching and research experiences, and our recent experiences of using the ToP in university classrooms and field research in Bangladesh, this paper argues that the implications of the ToP in university teaching and research are immense, but yet to explore through further research. Referring teaching to classroom instruction, research to scientific investigation dealing with human behavior, and the ToP mainly to its four-stage group process method known as ORID, this paper begins with the introduction of the ToP method followed by a discussion of the state of classroom teaching in schools/colleges, and the use of the ToP in university classrooms, and ends with the illustration of participatory research, and the application of the ToP method in the Bangladesh context.

Over the past fifty years of work in communities, organizations and classrooms through practical action research and applied learning, ICA (www.ica-international.org), a global organization concerned with human factor in development, has designed the ToP that enables groups to maximize meaningful engagement and to think and plan together effectively. The ToP method --- used by nonprofit organizations, government agencies, businesses, professional associations and communities from the early 1960s across the globe[1] --- includes three fundamental processes: focused conversation, consensus workshop, and action planning. This method enables groups in productive conversations, develop common ground for work and build effective short-range and long-range plans. The ToP practitioners and ICA staff have been engaged in human development work in more than 100 nations starting the use of the ToP in the Fifth City Project in the West Side of Chicago through international social change ventures, in the United Nations (UN) and World Bank programs, to hundreds of organizational and corporate change initiatives[2]. They also have published a number of books on different applications of the ToP[3]. The success conditions include five key or foundational values: inclusive participation, teamwork and collaboration, individual and group creativity, action and ownership, and reflection and learning.

The Focused Conversation Method - variably known as an art form method, a discussion method, an ORID method - is central to the ToP. A very practical and powerful tool, the ORID method facilitates children and adults to learn, makes learning meaningful in life, strengthens communication,

---

1 Umpleby, S., and A. Oyler. 2003. A global strategy for human development: The work of the Institute of Cultural Affairs. *Proceedings of the Annual Conference of the International Society for the Systems Sciences*, Crete, Greece, July.

Stanfield, B. 2000. *The Courage to Lead: Transform Self, Transform Society*. Toronto, Canada: Canadian Institute of Cultural Affairs.

Unpleby, Stuart, Medvedeva, Tatiana, and Oyler, Alisa. 2004. The Technology of Participation as a means of improving universities in transitional economies. World *Futures: The Journal of Global Education*, 6, 129-136.

2 Oyler, Marilyn, Gordon, Harper. 2009. The technology of participation. In Holman, Peggy, Devane, Tom, and Cady, Steven, The Change Handbook: The Definitive Resource on Today's Best Methods for Engaging Whole Systems: Easyread Super Large 24pt Edition (retrieved June 13, 2012 from http://books.google.ca/books?id=8UYsFOXiuKIC&printsec =copyright#v=onepage&q&f=false).

3 Bergdall, T. D. 1993. *Methods for Active Participation: Experiences in Rural Development from East and Central Africa*. Nairobi, Kenya: Oxford University Press.

Stanfield, B. 2001. *The Art of Focused Conversation: 100 Ways to Access Group Wisdom in the Workplace*. Gabriola Island, BC, Canada: New Society Publishers.

Troxel, J. (Ed.) 1993. *Participation Works: Business Cases from Around the World*. Alexandria, Virginia: Miles River Press.

Umpleby, S. 1989. Methods for community development: The work of the Institute of Cultural Affairs. (Available at www.gwu.edu/~umpleby/icaweb/.) Research Program in Social and Organizational Learning, The George Washington University, Washington, DC.

and solves problems individually and in groups[4]. It involves a whole-
system process using all the body's resources to come to terms with an
object or experience: the senses, memories and feelings. The four stage
progression of the thinking process includes questions that guide the group
through four levels of awareness: O – Objective: facts, data, senses: see,
hear, taste, smell, touch; R – Reflective: react to data, connect with reality,
heart: emotions, memories, associations; I – Intuitive: deeper connection
with reality, critical thinking, head: meaning, value, significance; D –
Decisional: take action, give meaning back to reality, action: resolution,
opinion, do something. The other techniques or processes under the ToP
are excluded in this discussion since those are basically the extension of
the ORID process.

While the purpose of teaching is supposed to facilitate learning,
no teaching and learning can occur without each other[5]. In case
of teaching without learning, participants may lose time, money,
potential gains in knowledge, cognitive development, and confidence
in themselves, or the education system. All teaching should strive
to create significant learning experiences, but the challenge is how
teachers or instructors do a better job of creating significant learning
experiences for students[6]. In the west a paradigm shift occurred in higher
education institutionally – the shift from 'teaching paradigm' to 'learning
paradigm'[7]. In the instruction paradigm, the mission of the educational
institution is to deliver instruction, to transfer knowledge from faculty
to students. On the contrary, the mission of the learning paradigm is to
produce learning, to create environments and experiences that elicit
student discovery and construction of knowledge. Unlike the former, the
method and product are not the same, and the means is not the end in the
learning paradigm. In the latter case, the teachers and students work in
teams; teachers develop every student's competencies and skills. In fact,
teachers play roles as facilitators. Students learn little by sitting in classes
listening to teachers, memorizing prepackaged assignments, and spitting
out answers, but they can learn much if they make what they learn as part
of themselves.

---

4 Nelson, Jo. 2001. The Art of Focused Conversation for Schools.: Over 100 ways to
guide clear thinking and promote learning. Gabriola Island, BC: New Society Publishers.
5 Nilson, Linda B. *Teaching at its Best: A Research-Based Resource for College Instructors.*
3rd Ed. San Francisco: Jossey-Bass, 2010.
6 Fink, L. Dee. *Creating Creating Significant Learning Experiences: An Integrated
Approach to Designing College Courses.* San Francisco: Jossey-Bass, 2003.
7 Barr, Robert B. and John Tagg. "From Teaching to Learning: A New Paradigm for
Undergraduate Education." *Change* 27.6 (Nov.-Dec. 1995): 13-25.

Active learning ensures participation. People learn or prefer to learn in different ways: learning or processing styles such as learning by doing hands-on activities, by reading or writing about a topic, by watching demonstrations and videos and by listening to a lecture[8]. Teaching involves various levels of intelligence. Traditional teaching is based mainly on verbal-linguistic and mathematical-logical intelligence. But there are many more – visual-spatial, kinesthetic or bodily, musical, intra- and interpersonal, and natural (Nelson, 2001). According to Howard Gardner's theory of multiple intelligence (*Frames of Mind*), everybody has intelligence, some forms of which are weaker and some stronger. Use of different learning styles such as active, verbal, visual, kinesthetic, cognitive, sensing, experiential and reflexive learning strategies has scientific currency in regard to effective student learning in higher education. Bloom's taxonomy of educational objectives includes three domains: cognitive (about knowing), affective (about attitudes, feelings), and psychomotor (about doing)[9]. Nelson (2001) illustrated that every step of the conversation method may involve different learning styles. One of the popular learning style models given by David Kolb can be illustrated here. At the O level, concrete experimental (CE) learning is used, at the R level , reflective observation (RO) style is used, at the I Level, abstract conceptualization (AC) style is used, and at the D level, active experimentation (AE) is used. According to Kolb, learners enter CE where they observe others and reflect on their own and other's experiences, and thereafter they proceed to RO. Later they attempt to assimilate their observations and perceptions into logical theories, thus moving into AC. When they use concepts to make decisions and solve problems, they exhibit AE.

Given the ToP's central focus on participation, let us discuss the state of student participation in Bangladeshi education institutions, based on our personal observation and experience as teachers. The system of education, and institutional constraints handicap participatory learning in this country. National education policy and its curriculum account for it because they leave little scope for group discussion and peer discussion. Students cannot participate in class discussion dominated mainly by instructors who often emphasize delivering lectures without bothering about whether or not students understand them. Instructors who lecture good are credited as good teachers. Naturally, they feel encouraged to deliver lectures only. Most teachers, if not all, do not encourage students asking questions even

---

8 Nilson, Linda B. 2010. *Teaching at its Best: A Research-Based Resource for College Instructors*. 3rd Ed. San Francisco: Jossey-Bass.
9 Teaching and Educational Development Institute (TEDI). 1996. Bloom's taxonomy if educational objectives. TEDI, The University of Queensland.

relevant to the topic of the class discussion. Neither do they focus much on the importance of using appropriate learning strategies. Therefore, while active, verbal, visual, kinesthetic, cognitive, sensing, experiential and reflexive learning strategies are applied and accepted worldwide, learners in Bangladesh get little space to apply all of those styles effectively. To specify, English language learners cannot adequately apply active, verbal, visual, and kinesthetic styles. Neither can they create interaction and make negotiation of meaning with their interlocutors in the class, which Richards (2006)[10] advocated for communicative language teaching. Thus, learner-instructor engagement is not properly ensured. But why is this non-interaction?

The answer is simple: the society and culture in which both instructors and learners are brought up want non-interaction and non-participation. Argument between instructors and learners in class is viewed as audacity in the society. Learners can say nothing against what instructors speak. Teachers cannot be questioned in the class. In this culture arguing with superiors is seen as impudence. Teachers are superiors, and therefore, students cannot argue with them in the class. Neither can they question their teachers. This traditional culture also does not approve questioning and arguing. Students culturally trained this way cannot question their teachers. Even at family or community levels, juniors by ages cannot argue with seniors on a topic, be it light or serious. Thus, participation is culturally but inadvertently discouraged in classrooms. Political culture also impacts education institutions, and in turn encourages non-participation learning. To mention, major political parties, their leaders, and policymakers are often non-cooperative, non-supportive, and non-interactive to each other. They lack the spirit of negotiation, discussion, cooperation, and participation. Their non-cooperation taste and tendency hampers the country to reach a consensus in national decision making. This non-cooperation culture in politics colonizes education institutions, inspires non-participatory learning, and thus, affects the learning health in classrooms. However, there other factors that also account for non-participation in classrooms, such as big class size but short span of class duration, inadequate resources including lab, libraries, internet connection, teaching staff, and administrative staff, and least freedom of instructors in designing lesson plans, the detailed discussion of which is excluded from the scope of the paper.

However, the focused conversation method and workshop method as formulated in the ToP earned a productive result while applied in teaching

---

10   Richards, J. C. 2006. *Communicative language teaching today.* Cambridge :
      Cambridge University Press.

the undergraduate students of criminology and police science department. At the beginning of the class students were given an ORID. They were seen to share their expectations and needs, and reflect at the end of the class on what they learnt, and their next steps. Though the syllabus or lesson plan was not designed based on the group consensus due to lack of institutional policies, and infrastructures, student feedback demonstrated significant engagement. Students found a difference in learning styles in the ToP from traditional learning. Students appreciated teaching styles and actively engaged in the discussion and problem-solving exercises. Same was the case with research.

To interview some key informants for a research project on police reform in Bangladesh, the questions were designed following the ORID of the ToP --- a group-based method that can gather information through asking sequential questions and processes and can help researchers understand and interpret social phenomena. In designing instruments for another research project on understanding Islamist militancy and terrorism in Bangladesh, ORID and workshop methods were used. In both research cases, the ToP gave participants an opportunity to respond in their own words, and the ability to evoke responses meaningful, culturally salient, rich explanatory, and unpredictable in nature. In addition to these academic and institutional researches, the ToP method was used to gather data for planning, monitoring and evaluation of two community projects. While research is essential for proper planning, implementation and re-planning, ORID and workshop method can provide very practical participatory tools to gather social facts and people's perceptions from the community of landless villagers, children and their guardians.

To conclude, the ToP is of immense value for student participation in active learning and participatory research. We applied this method as a test case in both colleges and universities, and got a wonderful response and good result what Nilson (2010), Fink (2003), Kobl (as cited in Nelson, 2001), TEDI (1996), and Barr and Taag (1995) suggest for active significant experiences. The ToP method allows the students to extend their real life experiences to a deeper interpretation and application. The ToP can be used in lesson planning as well as in the design of teaching strategy what Nelson applied to high schools. The education institutions, therefore, can adapt and apply the ToP method that stresses cooperation to devise solution, and earn a maximum outcome. This method also helps students develop qualities of facilitative leadership among themselves. A powerful tool for creative thinking and analysis, the ToP can be used in participatory research as means for collecting quality data from the respondents, engaging them in answering the structured and non-structured questions with providing ample space for a researcher being a neutral facilitator to clarify the ambiguity of the questions if needed. Despite the possibility and the positivity of the ToP, its success exclusively depends on adequate funding, appropriate polices and a strong mindset of the policy makers, leaders, and administrators, and after all, the change of education culture and system. However, further research is needed to explore the applications of ToP method in Bangladesh. The implications of ToP approach presented here can be particularly relevant to other South Asian countries where more or less similar education environment exists till today.

Developing Curriculum on Interdisciplinary Course on Training and Development

Robertson Work and Tatwa P. Timsina

1. Background:

In November, 2008 about 200 people from all over the world gathered in Takayama, Japan to participate in the 7th Global Conference on Human Development organized by ICA International jointly with ICA Japan. ICA has been conducting this type of conference in the theme of human development for the last 24 years. Since the early 50s, ICA has been working in the field of promoting human development globally.

In the thematic workshop held in Japan, participants identified various reasons for starting an academic programme on training and development. As ICA is working on human development around the world, the need for this type of programme was emphasized so that it could provide quality education in this field. The participants recommended that the course should provide curriculum modules in such a way that students would be able to build positive values, self esteem, human relation and innovation. Participants suggested that the students should learn about facilitation, participatory approaches, social artistry, negotiation and mediation skills, cultural awareness and thinking styles. They should build skills of artistic expression, conflict resolution, planning and project management, development methods propounded by ICA and others. Based on the ideas of the participants, a series of courses is being proposed. The list has been revised after thorough research on global and national efforts of developing human capacities in this area.

The rapid inflow of people in this field has led to myriad applications of participatory approaches. Starting from personal level improvement towards a positive outlook on life, the philosophy of participatory approaches has been applied to greater causes throughout the world. Many companies, government organizations, social services and community development organizations have successfully used such approaches and are enjoying benefits contributed by the approach. Further, many networks have based their activities on a participatory philosophy. Though in its very early stage, it has touched and made a positive impact in many lives.

Due to the ever-expanding applications of various approaches of participation, people are becoming more interested in facts that support this approach. People are interested in knowing through research and empirical methods the reliability of such approaches in different aspects. As we look to the future, the world we live in is certainly a better place with lots of positive energy surrounding us. Due to the positive impact of the proposed training and development programme, people will have an increased level of energy to do something better, to be someone better.

Nations have included participatory methodologies in planning, governance, development and education. Every nation is putting a substantial amount of budget in enhancing its strengths. The concept of multi-stakeholder involvement is integrated in the Nepali constitution so as to produce better results in the overall performance of the government.

As all organisations need competent trainer/facilitators, so far this need is fulfilled by people from not so relevant discipline. This programme aims to develop capable human resources for personal and organisational transformation as trainers and facilitators. The graduates of this programme may work as competent consultants in various sectors.

2. Purpose

The Masters in Training and Development is being offered as an interdisciplinary program that will produce graduates of profound knowledge, state-of-the-art skills and the capacity to apply effective training and development in the private, governmental and NGO sectors in Nepal and abroad for the sake of promoting sustainable human development.

3. Building Human Capacity through Training and Development

Some approaches which can be applied for personal and organisational empowerment and human development are the Technology of Participation (ToP), Appreciative Inquiry, Logical Framework, Open Space Technology, Participatory Rural Appraisal, Future Search, Social Artistry and Result Oriented Leadership and Management.

The **Technology of Participation (ToP)** is based on natural thinking processes and has been evolving since the late 1950s, extensively tested and refined in community and organizational settings around the world. Originally known as 'ICA Methods' it has been honed since the mid 1980's into an effective group of tools and processes for working with organizations and communities known as "ToP."

Appreciative Inquiry is a common and popular research field in both Personal and Organizational Development. In this approach people are asked to consider organizations not as "problems to be solved" but as "webs of strength linked to infinite power". Many institutions and organizations around the globe have incorporated Appreciative Inquiry methodologies in their regular meetings and conferences. The discussion on the positive core of the organization is always the first agenda in the meetings. More meetings are conducted on strength building of an organization and the 4-D cycle is the standard way the meetings are conducted.

The aim of **social artistry** as embodied in this program is to implement the current transition toward creative change and growth in many arenas and in ways that will encourage and prepare its practitioners to more effectively accomplish the goals of social development. Its goal is to provide significant shifts through a variety of trainings, cross cultural, human and cultural development, education in human and cultural capacities and potentials, and other activating factors aimed at directing both individuals and social capital toward the creation of better societies and people.

Leadership and management are vital to make and manage change and are enablers of development, yet the investment in this sector is very low as compared to physical infrastructures. For example, banks are established but their management is often neglected. Resources spent on management development are mostly taken as 'expenses' rather than 'investments'. One of the main reasons management development is perceived as expense is the difficulty in establishing the direct link between the resources spent on management development and the result it can be attributed to. It is a complex undertaking but not unattainable.

The **Logical Framework Approach** is an analytical tool for objectives-oriented project planning and management. It has two main components - Analyzing the situation including participation analysis, problem analysis, objectives analysis and alternatives analysis. The second part includes designing the project, project elements, external factors and indicators.

4. Designing the Curriculum:

The initiation of this programme is aimed to fulfill the need to produce enough competent human resources who are equipped with knowledge and skills of training and development issues. The course is designed in such a way that the students will be able to provide quality service in this field. The teachers and students that are involved in the teaching-learning process also help to increase the awareness of the approaches among the communities in which they work.

This curriculum is designed to equip students to become facilitative leaders who are employable and self-sustaining for their families, effective in helping communities in their self-development, and who can take a leadership role in many aspects of regional civic engagement. This two-year curriculum has many elements, all of which are compatible with adult education best practices, and cover the different aspects of education.

5. Course Structure

The programme follows the credit system. Each course is assigned to a certain number of credits depending generally upon its lecture, tutorial and practical work hours in a week. In theoretical subjects one lecture per week is assigned to one credit as a general rule and is equivalent to a 16 hour lecture course in one semester.

The course comprises a total 60 credit hours spreading over four semesters with the following distinct components (as seen below). The normal duration for completing the course is two years.

Career Opportunities

Graduates of this course are needed in Human Resource Development departments of different organizations such as private companies, government training centers, NGO training and community development programs, international development agencies projects and training divisions and in organizational development consulting firms. The graduates may also develop their own organization as a freelance trainer/ consultant. Since the programme is interdisciplinary, there is scope of future career development in various fields.

Teaching Methodologies

Teaching methodologies will be highly interactive combining theory with practice, the conceptual with experiential and the rational/scientific with artistic/intuitive. Classes will include student conversations, faculty presentations, class reflections, faculty demonstrations of methods, small group practice sessions, field work and preparation of analytical papers.

Structure and Duration of the Course

The Masters in Training and Development is a 60 credit hour, four semester course to be completed within the period of two years.

Semester I: **Expanding & Deepening Personal Awareness and Values** (Who am I *becoming* as a training and development practitioner and how do I enable the personal development of others?) 16 Credit Hours

Semester II: **Learning Transformational Leadership Practices** (How do I practice *skillful means* of training and development?) 18 Credit Hours

Semester III: **Applying Awareness and Skills in Sustainable Human Development** (What are the human and natural *systems* in which training and development need to take place and how do I *apply* my knowledge and leadership skills within communities, organizations and institutions?) 14 Credit Hours

Semester IV: **Creating New Knowledge in Training and Development and Designing New Projects, Programs or Policies** (What is my unique *contribution* to the literature and practice of training and development that will further sustainable human development?) 12 Credit Hours

6. Course Outline

1st Semester of 1st Year 16 Cr. Hours	2nd Semester of 1st Year 18 Cr. Hours
Expanding & Deepening Personal Awareness and Values	**Learning Transformational Leadership Practices**
-PAV 111.3 Psychology of Learning -PAV 112.3 Training for Social Transformation -PAV 113.3 Training in National & Global Development -PAV 114.3 Values & Ethics in Adult Education -PAV 115.2 Adult Education -PAV 116.2 Training for Self Management & Development	-TLP 121.3 Technology of Participation -TLP 122.3 Social Artistry Leadership -TLP 123.3 Appreciative Inquiry & Other Facilitation Tools -TLP 124.3 Human Resource Development Training and Education -TLP 125.3 Conflict Transformation & Peace Building -TLP 126.3 Media, IT & Social Networking

1ˢᵗ Semester of 2ⁿᵈ Year 14 Cr. Hours	2ⁿᵈ Semester of 2ⁿᵈ Year 12 Cr. Hours
Applying Awareness and Skills in Sustainable Human Development -SHD 211.3 Cultural, Educational & Social Change -SHD 212.3 Business & Industry Training Methods -SHD 213.3 Participatory Governance -SHD 214.3 Sustainable Environment & Renewable Energy (select one practicum below) -SHD 215.2 Community Development -SHD 216.2 Organizational Development -SHD 217.2 Institutional and Systems Development	**Creating New Knowledge in Training and Development and Designing New Projects, Programs or Policies** -THC 221.2 Advanced Research Methodology -THC 222.2 Field Practice or Training Internship -THC 223.2 Seminar in Training & Development -THC 224.6 Thesis

Course Descriptions:

Semester I of Year I

Expanding & Deepening Personal Awareness and Values (Who am I becoming as a training and development practitioner and how do I enable the personal development of others?) 16 Credit Hours

PAV 111.3

Psychology of Learning (Self Awareness and Developing the Inner Self) [3]

The course enables the student to engage in a depth psychological exploration of his/her fundamental nature and out of this exploration to construct a new self story and image in line with the way life is. The course includes study of the nature of the self, the neurological perspective, self exploration, the review of and creation of self stories, exploring values for inner beauty, positive psychology, review of identities and roles, the quest for self realization, the possibility of self transcendence, impermanence and the realization of happiness and joy in this life. The course provides the groundwork for becoming a self-aware and self-reflective world-server.

PAV 112.3

Training for Social Transformation (Awareness of Others including the Community, Family and Society) [3]

The course takes the student on a journey of profound sociological reflection on the varieties of human beings and other forms of life and equips the student with the awareness and knowledge of the unique needs and possibilities of each being. The course includes the study of humanity and humanness, the lives of other species, gender and sexuality, age and developmental stages, ethnicity and race, culture and religion, exploring common values for global good, teams and partnerships, families, villages and cities, and nations and regions. The course provides the inter-active awareness necessary for effective development practice.

PAV 113.3

Training in National and Global Development (Evolution & History) [3]

The course expands the consciousness of the student to encompass a world-centric perspective within the scope of evolution and history. The course includes the study of planetary society, global culture and religion for human friendly planet, global plans and priorities, humanness and development, systems thinking, economic trends and dynamics, political trends and dynamics, cultural trends and dynamics, environment and energy trends and dynamics, social imbalances, analysis of current crises and opportunities including climate chaos, leverage and change strategies, the sustainable human development paradigm and innovative leadership styles to respond to this moment in history. The course sets current and future development practice in an expanded scale of time and space.

PAV 114.3

Values & Ethics in Adult Education [3]

The course provides the student with a deep investigation of past, present and future personal values systems in relationship to a world in need of development practice. The course includes a study of and reflection on the student's current personal values, ethical values throughout history, cultural values, religious values, national values, global values, universal values, positive and spiritual inquiry for strengthening a human friendly society, human rights, gender equity and includes practice of the student's newly constructed and internalized set up personal values. The course prepares the development practitioner with an opportunity to review and reinvent a value system as a wellspring for world changing.

PAV 115.3

Adult Education [3]

The course enables the student to set in motion life-long learning outside of formal educational and training situations, thus allowing the development practitioner to learn from any and every situation, encounter and experience. The course includes the study and practice of reflection, reflection-in-action, action research, learning by doing, learning theories, dialogue and interviewing, depth listening, ongoing personal study, model building, pattern seeing and mind changing. The course allows development practice to be a self-organizing, self adjusting process that continuously renews the practice itself based on new experiences and insights of a "learning self."

PAV 116.3

Training for Self Management & Development (Personal Practices) [3]

The course provides an unparalleled opportunity to learn about and to practice a comprehensive, integrated set of processes of self-management, stress management, success management and ongoing personal development. The course includes the study and practice of health, exercise and diet, meditation and yoga, use of myths, rituals and symbols, kindness, generosity and service, journaling, use of information technology and social networking for personal development, time management and stress relief. The course prepares the development practitioner to care for her/himself continuously thus providing renewal, refreshment, new vigor and insight in serving communities, organizations and institutions.

Semester II of Year I

Learning Transformational Leadership Practices (How do I practice skillful means of training and development?) 18 Credit Hours

TLP 121.3

Technology of Participation (3)

The course equips the learner with state-of-the-art facilitation techniques of the world-renown Technology of Participation. The course includes the study and practice of focused conversations and dialogue methods, workshop and consensus building approaches, historical and environmental scanning, strategic planning, participative action planning, advancing participatory methods, maneuver building methods, model building and scenario merging, leading productive meetings, preparing and making effective presentations, conducting organizational transformation, the image-behaviour linkage, team building, personal and group motivation, fostering of values and social responsibility, event planning methods and space designing. The course provides a set of integrated skills of facilitation that can be used to transform any community, organization or institution.

TLP 122.3

Social Artistry Leadership (3)

The course instills in the learner a wide range of creative processes for development practice that are designed to release the full potential of individuals and groups. The course includes the study and practice of the social artist in the world today, human capacities training and development, organizational systems and systems thinking, social psychology, appreciative leadership, mediation and group dynamics, cultural deepening and cultural change, creating community and strengthening civil society, processes and exercises of transformation of individuals and groups, and the use of art in development. The course provides effective techniques of the art of social change that can deepen and accelerate human development in organizations and communities.

TLP 123.3

Appreciative Inquiry and Other Facilitation Tools (3)

The course equips the learner with several of the most effective facilitation techniques available world-wide. The course includes the study and practice of Appreciative Inquiry, Emotional Intelligence, Spiritual Inquiry for Common Good, Asset bsed Community Development, Integral Analysis and Design, Whole Systems Design, Open Space Technology, Future Search, Participatory Rural Appraisal, Results Oriented Leadership and Development and the Logical Framework. The course presents a comprehensive tool kit for the development practitioner offering a range of diverse approaches to assist in community, organizational and institutional transformation.

TLP 124.3

Human Resource Development Training and Education (3)

The course transfers to the learner state-of-the-art methods of training and education for individual transformation in a variety of settings. The course includes the study and practice of human resource development, training needs assessment, imaginal education (image change), curriculum designing, course dynamics and flow, methods of presentation preparation and delivery, group discussion methods, workshop techniques, group reflection, demonstration of approaches, report writing, use of art forms in education (e.g., poetry, music, dance, theatre), mentoring and coaching, knowledge management and training evaluation. The methods learned can be used to train people in NGOs, business, government and neighborhoods in virtually any topic.

TLP 125.3

Conflict Transformation & Peace Building (3)

The course equips development practitioners to assist groups in negotiation and to help resolve conflict situations before, during or after conflict. The course includes the study and practice of negotiation techniques, clarification of positions, establishing common ground, give and take vs win-win solutions, fostering of trust and suspension of disbelief, types of conflict, dialogue methods and engaging in peace processes. The course provides essential knowledge and skills for transforming potentially dangerous and tension filled situations and leading to lasting changes in perception and behavior by those participating.

TLP 126.3

Media, IT and Social Networking (3)

The course provides formation of development practitioners who are expert in the use of media, IT and social networking for transformation of communities, organizations and institutions related to a variety of sectoral and thematic areas. The course includes the study and practice of image change, use of metaphor and story, use of language, framing of issues and solutions, analysis of audiences, types and use of media, types of IT, message creation, production, types and use of social networking, campaigning, social mobilization, IT and Globalization, use of spokespersons and champions and strategies of changing perceptions, attitudes and behavior. The course is a powerful induction into modern approaches and techniques of cultural change.

Semester I of Year II

Applying Awareness and Skills in Sustainable Human Development (What are the human and natural *systems* in which training and development need to take place and how do I *apply* my knowledge and leadership skills within communities, organizations and institutions?) 14 Credit Hours

SHD 211.3

Cultural, Educational and Social Change (3)

The course enables the learner to conduct effective cultural, social and educational change interventions applying the knowledge and skills from the previous two semesters. The course includes the study and practice of the dynamics of culture and religion, the re-creation of myths and stories, the use of rituals and symbols, applications of Social Artistry, the dynamics of education, language and life styles, health systems improvements, cultural evolution, applications of media and social networking in cultural change, message creation, campaigning and social mobilization. The course includes advanced theory but emphasizes practical applications of depth awareness and transformative facilitation at the community, national and international levels in projects, programs or policies.

SHD 212.3

Business and Industry Training Methods (3)

The course provides an opportunity to apply knowledge and skills learned previously to successfully achieve various aspects of business development. The course includes advanced theory and practical application related to economics, fiscal systems, market analysis, product and service development, business planning, corporate responsibility, equitable capitalism, staffing, finances and investment, marketing and selling, customer care, business negotiation and research and development. The course prepares the learner to develop his/her enterprise and/or to enable other individuals to do so as well as the larger society in its overall economic development.

SHD 213.3

Participatory Governance (3)

The course provides an opportunity for the emerging development practitioner to understand more deeply how to promote participatory governance at various levels and in many different institutions. The course includes advanced theory and practical application of leadership tools related to concepts of governance, governance actors, governance institutions and processes (e.g., executive, legislative, judiciary, accountability and transparency, human rights), institutional development, decentralization and local governance and urban and rural governance. Through this course the learner can test strategies to catalyze shifts in attitude and behaviour related to the promotion of good governance at local, national and international levels.

Certain parts of this courses are available in ICA Canada's Community Development Intensive.

SHD 214.3

Sustainable Environment & Renewable Energy (3)

The course presents advanced theory with an emphasis on practical applications of tools and awareness in promoting sustainable environment and renewable energy. The course includes the study and practice of ecology, principles of sustainable environment, environmental protection, natural resource management, climate chaos, climate change mitigation, and adaptation and the promotion of renewable energy development of hydro, solar, wind and geo-thermal. The course acts as a laboratory for the learner to experiment with sustainability strategies at the community, organizational or institutional level.

The learner selects one of the three courses below:

SHD 215.2

Community Development Practicum (2)

The course aims to provide the learner with an action laboratory for applying her/his new skills and knowledge in the field of community empowerment and development. The course includes advanced theory with an emphasis on practical application related to community development approaches, historic and geographic analysis, community assets, building a framework of support, long range visioning, systemic and underlying blocks, strategy development, partnership and coalition building, fund raising, proposal writing, project planning, program management and implementation, tracking and coordination, documentation and evaluation and development extension and replication. The learner will select a local urban or rural community in which to assist the local leadership with the development of their community. The student will analytically document success and failure of this effort.

SHD 216.2

Organizational Development Practicum (2)

The course is a learning laboratory for the student to experiment with applying the skills and knowledge acquired previously in the development of a selected organization within the NGO, business or government sector. The course includes advanced theory and practical application related to organizational development methods and strategies, organizational transformation, interviewing and story creation methods, organizational culture, organizational learning, creating Communities of Practice, consulting processes, use of various facilitation options and leadership development. The course allows the emerging development practitioner to learn by doing while being of service to an existing organization. The learner will document success and failure of this effort within an analytical framework.

SHD 217.2

Institutional & Systems Practicum (2)

The course is a living laboratory for the testing of skills and knowledge related to development practice within an institutional or systems setting. The course includes advanced theory and practical application related to integral four-quadrant theory, integral analysis and design, concepts of institutions, institutional design and implementation, systems theory and whole system design application. The course allows the learner to undertake action research while acting as a consultant to an actual institution or system. This will also emphasise the poverty alleviation and sustainable development measures.

Semester II of Year II

Creating New Knowledge in Training and Development and Designing New Projects, Programs or Policies (What is my unique *contribution* to the literature and practice of training and development that will further sustainable human development?) 12 Credit Hours

THC 221.2

Advanced Research Methodology (2)

The course will involve the learner in the study and practice of advanced research methodologies. The course will include a variety of conceptual frameworks, action research methods, participatory research techniques, methods of analysis, processes of synthesis, statistics, qualitative, quantitative and mixed indicators, interview techniques, report writing and bibliography guidelines.

THC 222.2

Field Practice and Training Internship (2)

The course involves the learner in field practice and training internships in a local rural or urban community project or a program of an organization of the NGO, business or government sector.

THC 223.2

Seminar in Training & Development (2)

The course provides an opportunity for each student to share her/his own analytical research paper with other learners related to a project, program or policy in the community, NGO, business or government sectors.

THC 224.6

Thesis (6)

In the last (4th) semester of the Masters program, each student carries out an independent research work and prepares a Thesis Report on the basis of his/her own original research findings with descriptive and/or scientific research design and methodologies. For the Masters in Training and Development the learner will create new knowledge related to the course of study and/or design an innovative project, program or policy that promotes sustainable human development within communities, organizations, institutions or systems.

7. Conclusion

There is a huge concern of promoting human capacity building and many organizations and individuals are contributing in this area. There is a need for national as well as global efforts in fulfilling this concern which requires support and collaboration from all levels. ICA in the past five decades has always strived for to do this and it is now the time to institutionalize this dream of developing human capacities for the 21st century.

Starting a programme like this will require support and cooperation from various individuals and organizations. We request all concerned to help realize their vision of developing human capacity through this programme.

By implementing this programme, it is expected that we will not only be able to produce the required human resources but also to realize the decades long vision of ICA of developing competent trainers and facilitators needed for different areas. By developing such human resources, we can bring multidimensional impacts contributing to the overall development of the nation of Nepal, Asia and the world.

Empowering Nepalese Civil Society through Civil Society Index – The Case of Nepal

Tatwa P. Timsina, PhD and Kushendra B. Mahat

Background:

After the revival of democracy in 1990, Nepal has experienced a huge increase in the number of Civil Society Organisations (CSOs). Informal sources indicate that so far more than 40 000 NGOs have been established and many have been affiliated to Social Welfare Council in Nepal.

In a country with a long history of autocratic rule, it is not surprising that civil society's influence on governance is limited. However, civil society is playing a leading role in empowering citizens, particularly among the marginalized groups. CSOs in Nepal are active in diverse fields such as poverty alleviation, community development, environment, human rights, conflict management etc. Many CSOs are also active in protecting cultural identities and heritage and many of such CSOs are also active in the remote part of Nepal.

Both the national and international CSOs are channeling resources for development. Nepalese CSOs have demonstrated their capability by spearheading development activities during the difficult period of conflict. They were able to cater the services even in the areas, where government presence was virtually negligible. Despite the increasing role of Nepalese CSOs, the fate of CSOs in Nepal is still not clear. Because of the lack of clear cut policies and laws on CSOs, there is much concern for the sustainability of CSO's activities in the country.

During the restoration of democracy, the civil society played an active role in raising voices against the autocratic regime. They have boldly raised their voice against corruption, organizing publicity and awareness programmes to curb corruption in the country (Dahal and Timsina, 2007). This has also caused many people and organizations to instigate activities against CSOs and draw attention of the government for limiting the role of CSOs.

The history of modern CSOs in Nepal is not a very long. During the royal regime, social service work was entirely in the hands of the government or elite group closed to the ruling government or royal family. However, if we trace the history of collective actions for various developmental activities, we may find the existence of civil society activities from time immemorial.

The restoration of democracy and multiparty political system in 1990 was a great turning point for the CSO sector, which created an era of civil society development in Nepal. The process of establishing NGOs became simple even for ordinary people. Any group of people with at least nine members may apply for CSO registration with rules and policies in the form of organisational constitution in the format suggested by the District Administration Office (DAO). Such organisation may work anywhere in the country with the support of any donor.

Civil Society Organizations in Nepal

The dictionary meaning of the 'Civil Society" is human society or the living together. But in the broader term it means that most citizens will behave responsibility of their own free will. Responsibility means that not just minding one's own business but rather being actively concerned with the fate of society as a whole. CIVICUS has defined civil society as "the arena, between family, government, and market where people voluntarily associate to advance common interests".

After the Second World War, the momentum gathered towards the development of a civil society. Freedom from the colonial era and the process of democratization began with a new vigor and purpose. Civil Society can be difficult to understand, because there are a number of conflicting definitions. There is a widespread agreement that during the past few decades, civil society receded and political/ commercial society advanced in terms of their impact on people's lifestyle.

Civil society in Nepal encompasses non-state, non-governmental, voluntary people's forum, organizations and movements organized from below. Civil society is a space for popular forces, the majority of people, for the recomposition of their capacity to imagine, organize and develop their identity and bring real progress in the life of a majority of the population (Bongarts and Dahal, 1996). Civil society is a multitude of autonomous human associations, identities, networks and movements forged for the sake of protecting themselves from the arbitrary and unjust decisions of the holders of power and wealth and promoting their rational self-interest

(Dahal, 2001).

The demands and aspirations of people who expect to fulfill their shared interests, join if the government and other formal sectors are unable to do so. People with common interest and common justice may gather to form a civil society aiming to improve the society they are concerned for.

Civil societies in Nepal have shown their presence in various fields such as human rights, environment, forestry, irrigation, self-governance etc. In Nepal, civil society's concern is more towards meeting the basic needs of the people.

Civil society can play an active role in mobilizing capability of human resources available in the area which helps transforming the community. Civil society can also play the role of watchdog in transition society. It must build trust in the society as a clean and honest organization with no political ambition or prejudices.

CSI Initiative in Nepal

Civil Society Index (CSI) is an action-research project that assesses the state of civil society in countries around the world, with a view to creating a knowledge base and an impetus for civil society enhancement initiatives. It also actively involves and disseminates its findings to a broad range of stakeholders including governments, media, donors, academics and the public at large.

ICA since its inception has given emphasis on strengthening civil society globally. As an active member of CIVICUS, many ICAs around the world are playing an active role in implementing CSI, thus rekindling its historical mission.

ICA Nepal with the technical input of CIVICUS: World Alliance for Citizen Participation carried out an action research on 'Civil Society Index of Nepal'. Civil societies have been playing active role to institutionalise democratisation process to service delivery since the restoration of democracy in Nepal.

ICA Nepal found the goal, vision and mission of CSI project much similar with its organisational goal. ICA Nepal as an executing organisation for civil society index (CSI) started the work from April, 2003.

CIVICUS provided technical support to ICA Nepal like rendering a toolkit, describing in detail the implementation process, selecting us as a national coordinating organisation and giving an opportunity to take part in CIVICUS world assembly. With the support of CIVICUS, ICA Nepal prepared and updated a proposal on 'developing civil society index of Nepal' and put forwarded to different donors for the financial support. We were able to get partial support for this work as ICA also put matching amount for the project.

CSI – Assessing CSOs

The CSI defines civil society as "the arena, between family, government, and market where people voluntarily associate to advance common interests." Within this arena people "associate" with one another through a large and diverse array of formal and informal associations as organizations. For the purpose of the CSI, civil society organizations (CSOs) are used as a generic term to include all forms of peoples' associations within civil society, be they formal or informal. A major challenge in assessing civil society is to take account of this extremely broad range of CSOs, that represent very diverse groups/interests, exist at different levels and take on a variety of organizational forms.

A primary goal of the participatory CSI approach is to empower stakeholders through the promotion of dialogue, collective learning and network-building. It helps in:

- assisting civil society in identifying and addressing its strengths, weaknesses and priorities for action.
- developing an increased understanding of the civil society arena,
- providing information about civil society's contribution to broader social change,
- generating an indigenous civil society action agenda,
- increasing capacity, ownership and readiness to carry out specific interventions by indigenous civil society actors.

The CSI delivered the following outputs:

- A comprehensive, yet accessible report on the state of civil society in the particular country along civil society's main dimensions, namely its structure, external environment, values and impact;
- Specific strengths and weaknesses of civil society in each of the four dimensions,
- Key priority areas for civil society intervention,
- A meeting ground for civil society stakeholders,

- A visual map of civil society,
- Cross-country comparisons of the state of civil society,
- Sharing of successful civil society strengthening initiatives,
- An international network of civil society practitioners and researchers.

Framework and Research Methodology

The Index was designed to assess four different dimensions of civil society: (1) the structure of civil society, (2) the external environment in which civil society exists and functions, (3) the values held and advocated in the civil society arena, and (4) the impact of activities pursued by civil society actors.

In order to obtain a picture of the overall state of civil society, the project assessed and scored (on a scale of 0 to 3) the four identified dimensions of civil society. Each dimension is, in turn, made up of several sub-dimensions.

Structure: (1) Breadth of citizen participation, (2) Depth of citizen participation, (3) Diversity within civil society, (4) Level of organisation, (5) Inter-relations, (6) Resources

Environment: (1) Political context, (2) Basic freedom & rights, (3) Socio-economic context, (4) Socio-cultural context, (5) Legal environment, (6) State-civil society relations, (7) Private sector-civil society relations

Values: (1) Democracy, (2) Transparency, (3) Tolerance, (4) Non-violence, (5) Gender equity, (6) Poverty eradication, (7) Environmental protection

Impact: (1) Influencing public policy (2) Holding state and private corporations accountable, (3) Responding to social interests, (4) Empowering citizens, (5) Meeting societal needs.

The scoring exercise was carried out by a 'jury' of informed citizens. Each indicator, sub-dimension and dimension scored from 0 (most negative) to 3 (most positive). For each indicator, four universal qualitative scenarios had been developed to provide substantive meaning to these categories. Scoring was based on the available secondary information and the data gathered through primary research.

THE FINDINGS:

The diagram of the Civil Society Diamond for Nepal showed that it is rather well-balanced and of medium size. The figure shows that the structure and values are in slightly better condition than the environment and impact. The scores vary from 1.3 to 1.7 indicating that the status of civil society in Nepal is almost at the middle and needs much improvement in all dimensions almost equally.

FIGURE 1: Civil Society Diamond for Nepal

Nepal

Structure

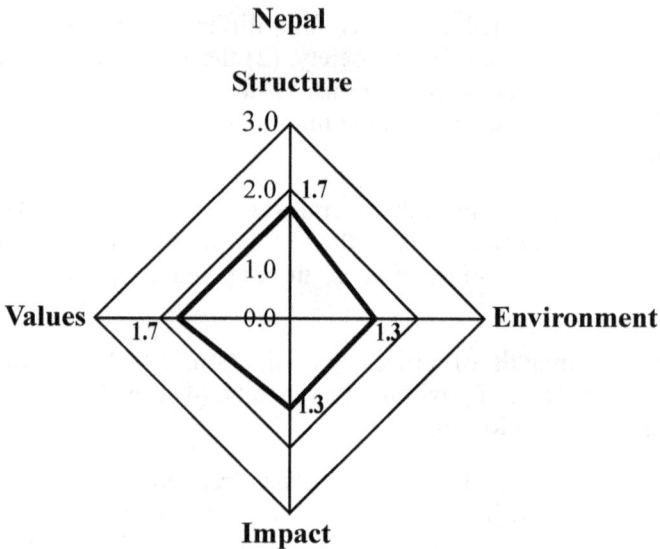

Impact

Summary of each dimension

Structure: Nepalese CSOs have demonstrated their strength in participating in non-partisan political activities by also participating in the movement to reinstate democracy. Participation of Nepalese people in global CSOs is nominal; CSOs in Nepal have very limited communication facilities and also have inadequate numbers of capable human resources. However, CSOs in Nepal are quite diverse and reflect the social, economic and political plurality of the country. CSOs are more urban-based and representation of different ethnic groups is unequal. Various other indicators such as 'existence of umbrella bodies', 'support infrastructure', 'international linkages', 'cooperation between CSOs' also show rather low scores. Financial and structural facilities for CSOs are nominal, and many CSOs do not even have their own office. This indicates that many CSOs in Nepal are working in a very difficult setting with nominal resources and physical facilities. The score of structure i.e., 1.7 indicates that there is a need for massive intervention to improve this aspect of the CSI Diamond. Despite the lower scoring in most of the indicators, Nepalese CSOs see promising and conducive socio-political conditions in future.

Environment: The Environment dimension of the CSI Diamond in Nepal is in a state of change. The analysis of the indicators produces a rather poor score for the environment dimension. One of the major disabling factors was the country's volatile political environment. The political rights of citizens were violated, CSOs were threatened and the state was almost on the verge of collapse. In the last few years, the political system of the country was changed several times which, in turn, directly affected the functioning of CSOs. Although in all political systems in the past, the regime emphasized full rights to people, in practice the respect and promotion of these rights varied drastically.

For about a decade because of the conflict, the country was in a chaotic situation. CSOs were threatened in rural areas. All the subdimensions such as political context, basic freedoms, socio-economic and socio-cultural context, legal environment, state-CS relations and private sector-CS relations showed a problematic stage. The overall situation in the last years was so negative that the regime lost control over about half of the country, corruption became rampant, press freedom was curtailed and the public lost hope. Despite such a harsh political environment, people did not lose trust, which enabled many CSOs to operate even in such a difficult period of history. Some CSOs tried their best to reach the most needy people and to create space for activism and to encourage respect for human rights, even between warring factions. The score for environment was low (1.3), indicating that CSOs went through a very difficult period.

Values: Nepalese civil society promotes and practices positive values only to a certain extent. The score for values dimension is 1.7. The study revealed that civil society is dedicated to practice of democratic norms not only within the organisations but also in society at large, with a view to supporting the democratization of the Nepalese society. It is also active in promoting transparency, non-violence, gender equity and environmental sustainability.

The report indicates that Nepalese civil society is still not so active in tackling corruption and financial transparency issues. It remains unable to instil a gender equity-friendly value system within organisations, and the role of CSOs in poverty eradication is still not very impressive. Ordinary citizens do not believe that CSOs were established mainly for fighting poverty, since CSOs have not yet been able to include this as one of their major values.

CSOs have played a central role in the restoration of democracy and peace. Although non-partisan political actions are dominated by men and only few CSOs are led by women, women's participation in community forestry and environmental improvement activities is increasing.

Impact: The study reveals that Nepalese CSOs have not been very successful in influencing public policies and exerting pressure on government and other decision-makers. This is reflected in the rather low score for the impact dimension (1.4). CSOs have partially contributed to empowering marginalized communities and getting basic services closer to the people. More specifically, CSOs have been working hard to support minorities, women and children. Moreover, CSOs role in supporting livelihoods has been rather significant and has made many people more interested in the role played by CSOs in social and economic development. In all the consultations, participants felt that without the participation of CSOs, the country will not achieve the Millennium Development Goals set by the UNDP and supported also by the government of Nepal.

The impact of CSOs in the promotion of human rights, drafting of social policies, and lobbying the state is not very strong. CSOs in Nepal are not very active in holding the state or private sector accountable. Nevertheless, the public trust in CSOs is quite high and this helps them to implement their activities in local communities in spite of numerous limitations.

CSI – Some Key Recommendations:

CSI has proposed a number of recommendations on empowering CSOs. Some of the major ones are as follows:

- Broaden awareness of citizens: CSOs should educate citizens about the changing nature of the national and local political environment, to continue promoting the values of democracy, peace, social justice and progress.

- Enhance internal capacity: CSOs should focus on developing internal capacity to carry out activities with greater impact. CSOs should promote professionalism and invest in training.

- Improve transparency: CSOs should improve internal transparency so that information is accessible to all citizens, not just direct stakeholders. More transparency will benefit their legitimacy, public ownership and participation.

- Government support: CSOs should lobby to get government support. At the same time government should establish a mechanism to work with CSOs. With the democratization of the state, political parties and public institutions, a more conducive environment will be created for civil society-state-market synergy.

- More cooperation within civil society: CSOs should collaborate and cooperate so as to maximize the impact of their work. They should identify areas where they have competitive advantages and expertise.

- Capacity-building and local ownership: International donors should focus on building the capacity of local and national CSOs in Nepal. INGOs should work through local partners. This would increase knowledge and expertise for local CSOs to address the causes of poverty, inequality, and conflict. Local people should be given preference during recruitment of the staff, setting of goals and priorities, implementation, evaluation and feedback for further reforms.

Conclusion

The CSI study emphasizes on the importance of CSOs in the overall development of the country. As this study is the first comprehensive analysis of civil society in Nepal, it will most probably start a phase of more in-depth analysis of the role that CSOs play in Nepalese society. ICA Nepal believes that not only CSOs, but also government, the private sector and the international community may benefit from the recommendations from whatever this study has identified. The findings of this study will also have a global relevance, as they are part of the CSI project, and can be used to analyse the status of Nepalese in light of an international perspective.

ICA Nepal is also committed to putting the recommendations into practice and facilitating the participation of other organisations in this endeavour. ICA Nepal believes that implementation of CSI recommendations help in empowering CSOs in the country.

Awakening Communities through Awareness and Education: ICA Japan's Approach - Past, Present, and Future

Wayne Ellsworth

It all began with a side trip after a TTL network meeting, I think that was in Lonavala in 1988. Shankar Jadhav took me to see Javale Village, and then back to his home in Pune. Javale was in pretty good condition thanks to many colleagues work for many years.

First we were introduced to seven villages (Malagon Cluster) about 70 kilometers northwest outside of then the relatively small city of (Poona) Pune. These seven villages were without water 9 months of the year and the villagers were living in broken down straw and mud huts. It would take a whole book to tell about what miraculous transformation took place for these villagers over the next several years. It seems so clear now, it seemed like just yesterday when they learned they had the right to at least 10% of the water that fell on their land, and eventually everyone came to help, everyone included businessmen, trust, government helpers, with the partnership between ICA Pune and ICA Japan keeping the energy and training to support the villagers.

Several years later, one of the newly provided water systems broke down, and it seemed like forever until they had a village meeting to decide what to do. Many were in favor to give the system to the government to fix when they could. A few discerning people remembered the broken promises made by politicians who came to the villages only just before elections, and said there must be a better way. After a very long time over the next several weeks of deep struggle, they came to the decision that they should not let go of their water system to let it fall into great disarray, but instead they would assess a small tax themselves, and unbelievably rapidly the volunteers repaired the water system, operating out of the **21st century**

168 • Changing Lives, Changing Societies
ICA's Experience in Nepal and in the World

concept of common good helping each other succeed.

While we were helping the fisherman recover in Chile, the team stopped to lead the fisherman's meeting which had a usual attendance of about 35. Leading with ToP, the meeting progressed very smoothly, and the result was an action plan they would begin cooperating on. After a while, I counted 85 men inside and some more outside. Why did all the fishermen come from? They heard the team was there, and for the first time, they were having creative energy instead of the usual fighting and no action!

We usually had the habit of going beyond where the regular aid was distributed. Often we were warned to not go beyond, with fear showing in their faces. Upon arriving the "fearful" places, we always were welcomed warmly by the kindest people ever. They were used to everyone bypassing them, and they had wonderful lives and great stories of proud self sufficient people, often with great histories. To me, they seemed more developed than busy urban people, and we appreciated the chance to give them a little aid. Similar left out circumstances were found in Aceh, Peru, Kenya, India, Nepal, and almost everywhere a disaster or famine struck. Often people had lost friends, families, businesses, or maybe they had very little to start with, and now were being faced with famine and dying children.

Much listening to their painful stories was required, and they invited us to facilitate simple workshops to recover their sense of pride and point them to the future full of elements their newly shared vision, and a trustworthy partner that was willing to help a little for a while.

How was this possible one might ask, going beyond, knowing no one in advance? The world now is tightly connected, and after many Skype out phone calls, we always became connected with people we knew years before, from some meeting or another. They went with us, or arranged for others to go to the ends of the earth, even where the roads were broken and the airports were in temporary facilities just opened the day we arrived!

For longer term projects, we provided transportation for ministry of agriculture people to leave their offices and go into the field to teach the people that they had insufficient budget to mobilize themselves, and rare cases we arranged computers so that they could produce a fine written report for us and our funding partner. In other cases, the local government workers sanctioned our projects, provided security, helped us deliver emergency supplies, turning the tension of chaos into joy-filled activities.

This is only a short introduction about what doing emergency aid or "development" is all about. It is not simple to convince the authorities to provide us with tax payers money, since they seldom leave their offices and really get to know real individuals.

Giving individuals and communities global relationships, facilitating their grasping their own vision, and speeding awakening to their fullest is at the core of ICA Japan's reason for being. We have a unique opportunity of being in the Land of the Rising Sun with its long history and now being in the center of the Universe with all of its destinal opportunities. For us, and for our funding partners, we sense a profound challenge at this point in history.

We have been a learning community and a maturing organization for 25 years of building global partnerships with Asia (Aceh, the Philippines, Vietnam, Pune in Maharashtra and Patna in Bihar India, Nepal), Africa (Kenya Mombasa, Saia, Kitui, Isinya, Turkana, Nigeria, Cote d'Ivorie, Zambia), South America (Haiti, Columbia, Mexico, Peru, Chile, Brasil), Japan (Tohoku, Western Japan, Northern Japan), and other places around the world. Some have been sustained relationships and other shorter term projects usually focusing on Emergency Aid.

ICA Japan, along with ever present local partners, have built training centers, irrigation systems, community gardens, livestock and dairy, community centers, women's development programs, vocational training, facilitated leadership training and community planning, planted hundreds of hectares of trees, provided emergency food, water, clothes, school buildings, pipelines, providing whatever was urgently needed to those who had not access to resources, and were too far from the comfortable centers where aid normally focuses.

While we have created this wide track record, we often think: what about the people, and what allows them to accept what we are offering, and make the changes that we introduce, and to continue to prosper? What happens when we leave and what would enable them to sustain the activities and make their environment a truly great model for others to follow and build upon? This is often an elusive question, and to find warm hearted people to provide this kind of help and to also write the reports and do Japanese style meticulous finances is even more elusive!

Now, what gives us vision and methods to apply, going beyond aid to really helping people help themselves? Over about 35 years individuals created a set of core competencies that are essential to our being. Since we are fabulously tied together as a global network, we continue to learn and develop as a disbursed community. I will introduce the core methods and models for you to comprehend what we are thriving upon.

Guiding Master Images

Two master images help us along the way. We could not quit when we get tired because we feel they are and will be keys to the success of great projects. In addition, reading a few revolutionary books enabled us to maintain our presence.

First comes to mind in that images change lives. In Kitui project, we took residents to a demonstration farm for a week, and as a result, one young man, upon returning from the visit, made the most impressive two hectare garden plot, much better than anyone had built in the two years of training that had been provided to the communities. Second, in Vietnam, they began replicating 100 fold the demonstration lake cleaning project. Images change lives.

ICA has well thought out models, which have evolved into technologies for development of communities, organizations, and individuals. Let me introduce my view of how the technologies have recently come together. It is quite simple, really. We have tended to lump everything into the Technology of Participation. This Spring, I felt that our Technology of Participation (ToP) could not present all of our knowledge well, and suddenly there a flash of lightning, and this model come forth. Basic is Technology of Community (ToC), born out of our half a century of living together as a community, and now as a global network. Out of community was born the Technology of Participation (ToP), which is the core component of most participatory processes. New on the horizon is the Technology of Spirit or ToS.

We have lived community, participation, and spirit since our foundations, yet now in the 21st Century they have emerged not only as awarenesses, but for me, all three have now emerged as technologies. Up until now we have fondly and for the simplicity of marketing called most of our

"curriculum" ToP. Above is what is for me the emerging model. This
makes room for discerning the full potential of each of the three, out of the
depths of the universe. As we further identify the key components of each,
we will succeed is teaching and spreading our wisdom faster and wider.

Awakening Communities

Now, you might ask, what has this to do with awakening communities?
Everything, especially as we make expand our projects and keep them
relevant to the rapidly changing times and trends. Since the ToS has recently
come to my attention, I'll expand on relevance of ToS in the conclusion.
This model is not jet ICA's consensus, but ICA Japan is testing for now .

Ever since our very beginnings, it was repeated over and over that what
happens to a single community makes little difference at all. Building
Awakened Attractor Communities is what we are all about, and our peer to
peer process makes this all possible. Helping someone, some community,
or organization has to be about transformation and attraction, that is the
bottom line. This begins with the individual and expands immensely. That
is how we build attractor communities, even where at first the people have
little or nothing. The economically poor communities are already attractor
communities! They have what counts most. They have love, compassion,
and take as little as possible from the environment. When we help those
communities, we are careful to not bring to them what they do not need.

I remember one time in Siaya Kenya we were invited to visit one person's
home. She lived in a square block of homes, with a courtyard in the center.
I was told that everyone living there had AIDS, and that perhaps included
some of the precious children playing happily in the courtyard. We in
to her home, and it was almost bare; she invited friends from across the
courtyard. After a while, they asked if we would like something to drink.
To be polite, we said "yes", and after some time, there appeared two
half glasses of cool orange juice – the last juice that anyone in this small
community had! I never forget how humble I felt after receiving the last
precious gift of orange aid love.

Transformation

Below is a helpful model "Capacities Necessary for Transformation".
When I use my imagination and place "electronic" with "information", I
can wait until an appropriate device becomes available. Soon iPads and
iBooks will make all that is necessary available, and without too many

distractions in terms of excessive games and monsters to take them away from a more meditative lifestyle. With a little imagination, you will understand the rest of this transformation model. To affect a community widely, one must do all five at the same time.

Capacities
Necessary for Transformation

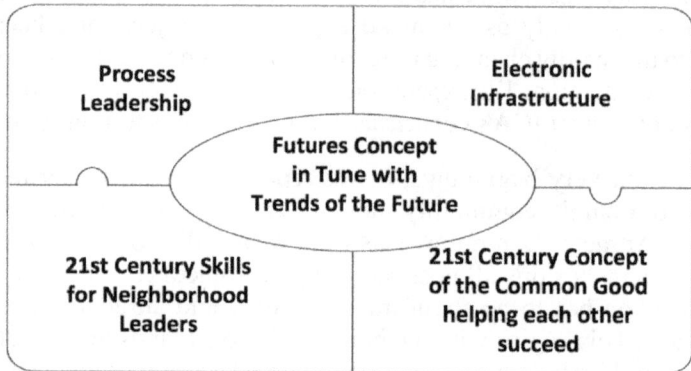

Process Leadership	Electronic Infrastructure
	Futures Concept in Tune with Trends of the Future	
21st Century Skills for Neighborhood Leaders	21st Century Concept of the Common Good helping each other succeed

Hanoi Environment Activities

A few examples of our efforts may be helpful. Over the past few years we worked in Hanoi cleaning a single small lake, using only natural water plants to devour the pollution in the lake. In facilitated planning sessions, there was a general lack of enthusiasm, and with the community around the lake, there was even greater skepticism, but we confidently proceeded.

This year we went back to Hanoi to renew the process. The plants had thrived and grown roots more than two meters deep, and the pollution was somewhat reduced. Surprisingly, everybody was now in favor, and we heard that the those who were in charge, were going to expand the floating natural floating cleaners to all 100 lakes in Hanoi. We cleaned up the broken down floats and provided a low cost replacement of about 8 floats with plants in their place.

What made this possible and successful, you might ask? It was the total team approach, and lots of time. In the beginning, we started by visiting a demonstration of this natural cleaning process in Chiba (East of Tokyo), and they were so certain of the floats, and they knew that Hanoi was famous for its (dirty) lakes, which also provided some resistance to flooding. After securing solid partners in Hanoi, and testing a variety of water plants, we held workshops with selected citizens from near the lake, and proceeded to place the floats into the selected lake. Time passed, but the Tokyo people kept in close touch. They even heard that several people had stayed on the floats, hidden in the tall plants, and fished in the cleaned up lake!

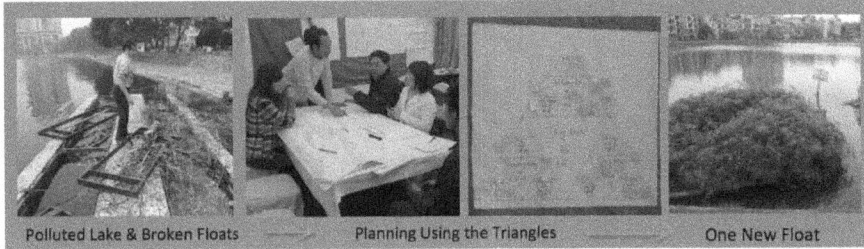

Polluted Lake & Broken Floats — Planning Using the Triangles — One New Float

Women's Empowerment in Mulshi, Pune, India

Beginning last October near Pune India, our JICA funded project in Mulshi focused on women's development. For three years they had been in the background supporting men's projects like irrigation, dairy, and bio-gas. The photo on the left shows women in the background somewhat listening to what is happening. Once their project got underway, they were actively engaged in training such as computer utilization, sewing their own clothes, and going about on field trips expanding their imagination towards their possible future. Also being introduced is hydroponics for the remotest village. As a consequence of year's of training and planning, people have stopped selling their land and some have returned to the village and its peaceful life.

Women in background — Computer Training & Pattern Making & Sewing

Kenya Drought Relief

Beginning last October 2011, Japan Platform (JPF) supported the project in Kenya focused on Drought Relief Aid for covering the five districts: Mandera at Kenya Somali border, Garissa, Magadi for Maasai people, South Horr and Loiyangalani. The intent is to support the smallest ethnic minority people in Kenya. Water piping, tank installation and food distribution for community and schools has given huge impact in the project areas, especially the northern part of Kenya, South Horr and Loiyangalani. Those places were forgotten for so many years, and women were walking 7 to 16km to fetch water, the children were suffering from hunger, some of the students couldn't even concentrate in their school because of food.

Pregnant women had to carry a 20L Geri-can on top of their head, and some times they drop the can on their foot, and the hospital is 100km away from their villages. After ICA Japan had installed almost 16km of pipes from their oasis and stream water, the women spend only 20 to 30 minutes to fetch water, some of them walk only a few meters to get clean water. Some of the over flow runs in to school garden and now the students are able to grow vegetables and plant trees. Food distribution for schools created awareness for the parents to take them to school since the school has food and water now. Community participation is very high, they like the way ICA works directly with the community and now they are planning to clean the bush around the water source to maintain clean water for their future.

Before the 19 km pipeline was finished

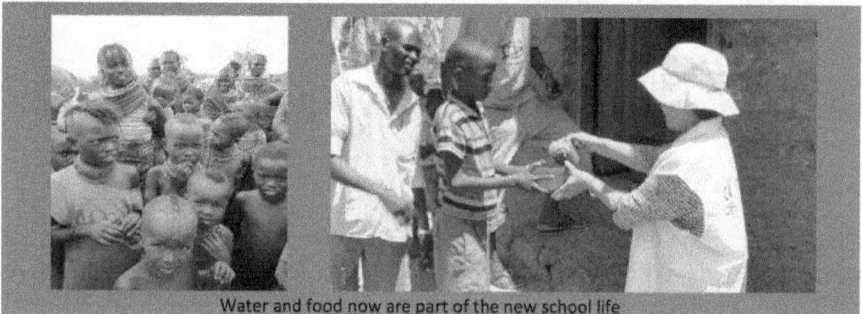

Water and food now are part of the new school life

Haiti Petit Guave Education Re-construction

The recovery of Haiti has been high on our priority list since the 8.8 earthquake happen, destroying most of the weak buildings, killing 300,000 people, and leaving more than 1,500,000 people homeless. The capital city was already over crowded and being reached by aid groups, consequently we went to an outlying town named Petit Guave, and began by delivering Emergency Aid funded by JPF, and making many acquaintances and long lasting friends.

The following year we discerned that the 120,000 people there needed much of their education system rebuilt, both in this city and in the surrounding mountainside. We built a "temporary" elementary school building with the aid of the enlightened bi-lingual Mr. Desgranges, much to the delight of students and teachers alike. It had seven classrooms and a combined teacher's room and administration office. There we had many complications due the contractor leaving before the construction before the building was completed, and we had to raise additional resources to complete the building.

Following this, the city of Hyogo Japan decided to fund a second similar building, for which we chose to place this building on the distant mountaintop overlooking Petit Guave, the bay, and much underdeveloped land. We had in mind Anastasia's model of living in a Place of Love with nature and beauty all around, where they can return to the pristine origins of humankind. The newly found contractor was from this area, and he wanted to do this building even better than our specifications! This time we followed our intuitions, trust, and much patience and this resulted in a the most beautiful place we have ever built. Come as visit them sometime, if you can find the school hidden amongst the hilltops!

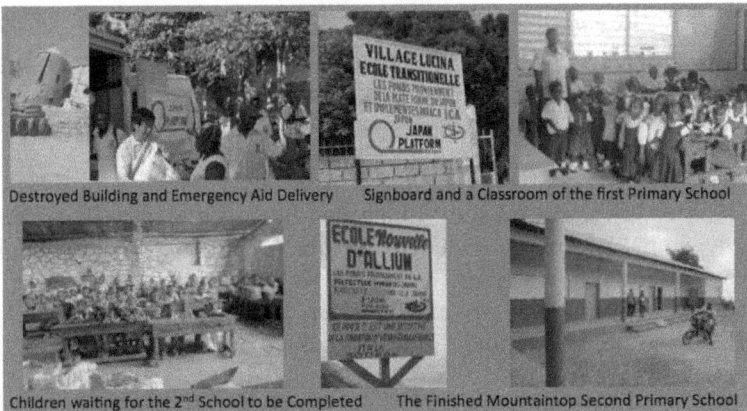

Destroyed Building and Emergency Aid Delivery   Signboard and a Classroom of the first Primary School

Children waiting for the 2nd School to be Completed   The Finished Mountaintop Second Primary School

Now we are facing what to do about the city below. We have built our replicable school far from the overcrowded urban complex. Listening carefully, we heard a huge cry for a small but modern vocational school for the unemployed youth. The initial design is for a two storey building on a small peace of Y shaped land, across from the mayor's office. We couldn't have found a more symbolic place if we had tried. Again, Mr. Desgranges guided us forward, and provided the land. Can you help us go forward with construction and creating the best up to date curriculum possible, keeping in mind Anastasia's insights for Creating another Space of Love?

Changu Narayan – Then and Now

For the last more than 12 years, with the support of ICA Japan, ICA Nepal carried out a series of developmental activities in Changunarayan Village Development Committee (VDC). ICA Nepal selected Changunarayan as its first project site in late nineties and since then carried out microfinance to education activities.

When ICA Nepal started the project work in this village, the village was having several problems such as illiteracy, lack of sanitation and drinking water, no any facility for lending money for income generation projects, untrained people etc. Thanks to the effort of ICAs from Nepal and Japan, within a decade time the whole village has been changed. Started from Rs. 50, the microfinance now has grown to more than 20 million Rs. The village has enough drinking water and almost everyone is able to read and write. Now, the local people are selling their products not only at the local area or nearby towns but also to faraway places like Korea. Many of the food products which are made by the local people are now exported.

ICA started the work following the basic ICA approach such as facilitating the community, involving them in the planning process, forming their taskforce and asking them to implement the activities. In this process, ICA Nepal simply worked as a facilitating organization.

Now, ICA Nepal's role in the village has been reduced as local people themselves are able to carry out all the activities. Most of the problems that we encountered before are now resolved and local people know how to tackle problems if they arise. Moreover, few new NGOs also came to the village and are continuing the work that we once started.

Changunarayan is a microcosm of intervention for human transformation.

It will be replicated to other disadvantaged area with similar background as well.

Tatwa P. Timsina, ICA Nepal

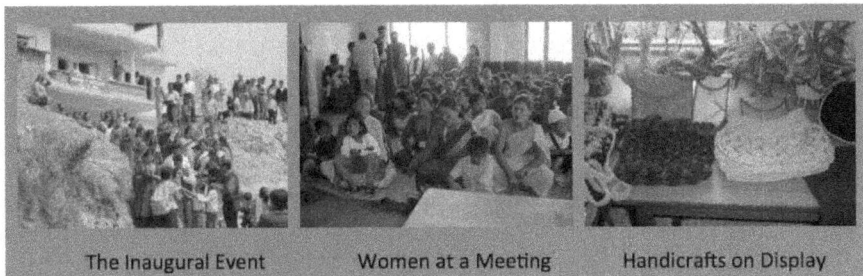

The Inaugural Event   Women at a Meeting   Handicrafts on Display

Tohoku Earthquake and Tsunami Recovery Projects

After the Earthquake and Tsunami on March 11, 2011, the data about the situation was: 15,170 people died, missing are 8,857, and evacuated people are 109,561 in shelters. Countless miles and miles of homes are completely destroyed, with most of the personal goods washed out to the ocean by the backwash. They have no Tsunami Insurance to recover their losses.

ICA decided to support 5 days after the Tsunami happened. Most people living at the shelters had lost families, houses and materials. We distributed water, portable cooking stoves, foods, flashlights, kerosene, toilet papers, and towels. It was so difficult to go the disaster place. Because there were no electricity, gas, water at hotels and anywhere at the disaster zone. We contacted the government and friends, asked them what do they need at that moment.

There were more than 2000 shelters from Iwate to Fukushima. One shelter had 700 to 1000 people. In March it was still cold, and people were without heaters. At shelters, they were bearded and hungry and cold. When we arrived at the shelters, everywhere there was not enough food and water. Shelter people were given a piece of bread a day. We knew several people who had participated to the ICA seminars at that area. In a beginning, we had collected materials in Tokyo as much as possible and delivered it.

Three months later, sheltered people were gradually moving to the temporary houses or rental rooms. The big problem was the mothers were afraid if their children might be affected by the accident of the nuclear radiation, which gave children at the nearby schools much suffering. They cannot open the windows nor play at school grounds. They wear masks and long sleeves to go to school. They are staying inside of the school because they have been warned many times about radiation, are severely afraid of the nuclear radiation affect. This was the third time ICA delivered food and household goods to Fukushima. We delivered beds, furniture, and cooking sets. They had to move to the temporary shelter houses at that time. So those materials were most welcome to the people who had to start house life again from the shelters.

We changed the target place from Sendai to Fukushima. At school, children needed air cleaners and fans, water purification systems. Many companies donated to us through JPF. We visited physical handicapped children home and donated coolers. They were so happy and still now we can talk with each other to exchange information.

Fish Foundation donated to the Fishermen Association a warehouse for a meeting room. People needed items very much as emergency aid before summer time. Americares hired ICA Japan to do much distribution as quickly as possible.

Now the Japanese government is busy to fix roads, pile up rubble, handling the emergency shelters, and building or repairing ships and settling the nuclear radiation. This will consume most of the money they have. What we need is artful communication and find out the vision of the life. They were amazed that so many people helped without even their name introduced. People just did what ever they could. Disaster was teaching us to help each other and discover nature's strong power which people had forgotten the secret power of nature.

Now we are preparing psychosocial aid such as arranging for people to clean forest paths, plant vegetables in greenhouses, and to vision and action planning to set their minds and hearts to the positive future.

Shizuyo Sato

Uplifting the Underdeveloped Villages in Madhepura, Bihar, India

Bihar is poor and one of the most backward states in development. This was worsened by the flood in 2008 when the huge earthen dam burst in Nepal, flooding for up to six months about a third of Bihar. This caused deep erosion in Bihar and covered much prime agriculture land with up to a half meter of stones and silt from the bottom of the dam.

ICA Japan visited in Oct 2008 for research, and when did a needs assessment in Jan 2010, the locals requested the construction of community centers for better communication in low caste areas, as well as training and capacity development. Consequently village based community development committees were established by women's self-help groups, farmers' groups, youth groups and teachers, regardless of caste. Low and high caste people and village's highest decision makers agreed to construct community centers on the low caste land so that locals can interact with and use the centers regardless of caste and to develop Madhepura area.

We jointly selected three villages which need community centers the most. The centers will be managed by the committee and the India counterpart with ICA Japan's guidance. In order to support further community development, we will hold workshops and training programs to nurture cooperation beyond castes, to raise the consciousness of the villagers, and to increase the villager's income. The variety of ten programs includes:

- Stakeholder seminars to acquaint people with the proposed activities,
- Community development seminars to give people awareness of the process of development, to understand local issues, find solutions, and to set action plans,
- Leadership training to nurture leaders who can solve problems and lead action plans,
- Agriculture training to improve crops of wheat, mustard, corn, banana, and mango
- Micro finance training for women's groups for art crafts, raising chickens, and herding animals,
- Youth vocational training in carpentry, sewing, and embroidery,
- Community disaster response training in skills such as how to communicate, where to evacuate, what to carry, and information sharing,
- Child care training for teachers to care for 500 children between the ages of 3 to 6,

- Sensitization through social dramas about health, education, environment, child rights, and to promote these,
- Management of the community centers its usage for such as wedding and study meetings.

We believe the villagers' lives will improve dramatically, their income will increase, and that their well being will strengthen. With a higher ability of villagers, we believe that the landowners respect and treatment of these villagers will also improve. It often takes about five years to make a substantial impact, and we plan to expand the program to ten villages with each having their own multi-purpose community center.

Land destroyed by the floods   One Multi-Purpose Center   Meeting with the community

Everlasting Principles for Community Development

Now I will present some core models that have continuously guided us and our colleagues on the adventure of awakening communities. The first is "Principles of Whole System Community Development". First is the introductory set and following page the harder to remember but complete set. There is a set of five principles of economic development, five principles of social development, and five principles of cultural development. In Zambia, these were painted full scale on the end of a large barn so that the whole community could be principled oriented.

The principles of Whole System Community Development which we used everywhere are:

Economic Principles:
- Consider the community as a self-sufficient unit,
- Circulate money quickly and continuously,
- Increase the community income,
- Retain money within the community

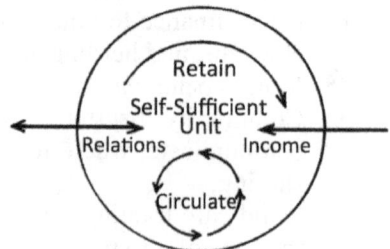

as long as possible,
- Relate to the external economy.

Social Principles:

- Operate within a clearly
delimited geography,
- Deal with all of the problems,
- Involve all of the people,
- Respond to the profound
human problem,
- Create and make visible key
social symbols,
- Cultivate towards the future.

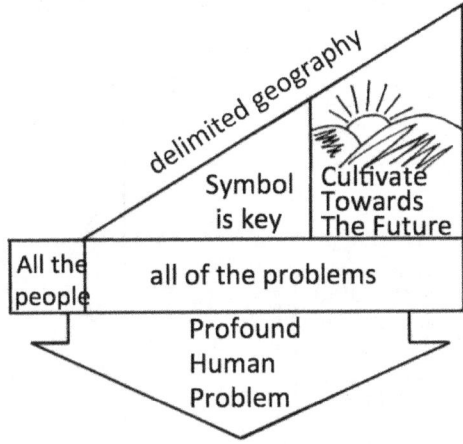

Cultural Principles:

- Rapidly create visible important
signs
- Deepen community commitment
- Recover community symbols,
- Reclaim a significant history,
- Exceed local boundaries. (CNN:
Go beyond borders)

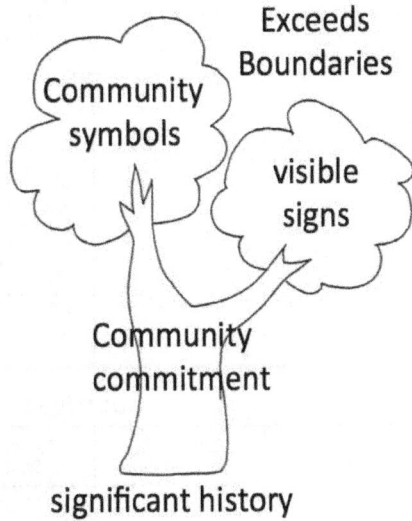

Principles of Whole System Community Development

ECONOMIC PRINCIPLES				
Self-Sufficient Unit	Increase Income Levels	Retain Money In the Community	Circulate Money	Relate to External Economy

SOCIAL PRINCIPLES				
Delimited Geography	All the Problems	All the People	The Profound Human Problem	Symbol is Key

CULTURAL PRINCIPLES				
Visible Signs	Community Commitment	Community Symbols	Significant History	Exceeds Boundaries

Comprehensive Community Development Programs

ECONOMIC DEVELOPMENT	CULTURAL DEVELOPMENT	SOCIAL DEVELOPMENT
FARMING SYSTEMS	**ENVIRONMENT**	**PREVENTIVE HEALTH CARE**
Diversity of Crops and Fishery	Improved Housing	Nutrition
Soil Conservation	Public Buildings	Primary Health Care
Water & Irrigation Systems	Public Services	Public Health Care
Appropriate Mechanization	Access Roads	Public Education
Livestock and Fish	Public Parks	Child survival
Agroforestry	Community Beautification	Preventive Medicine
APPROPRIATE INDUSTRY	**COMMUNITY ORGANIZATION**	**FUNCTIONAL EDUCATION**
Light Industry	Community Participation	Formal Education
Handicrafts	Community Promotors	Life Long Education
Cottage Industries	Community Workdays	Technical Training
Product Processing	Process Leadership	Youth Training
Non-Conventional Energy	Forms of Organization	Educational Communication
Repair and Recycle	New Organizational Training	Consciousness Education
COMMERCIAL SERVICES	**IDENTITY SYSTEMS**	**FAMILY WELL-BEING**
Marketing	Community History	Early Stimulation
Consumer Cooperatives	Customs and Traditions	Advancement of Women
Savings and Loan Systems	Celebrations	Community Youth Services
Transportation	Art, Music	Child Welfare
Cooperative Organizations	Information & Communicaton Means	Senior Citizen Care
Other Commercializations	Attractive Architecture	Family Life Education

Technology of Participation (ToP)

Almost every community is greatly enhanced and cultivated securely towards the future by carefully tailoring and facilitating a ToP Workshop such as:

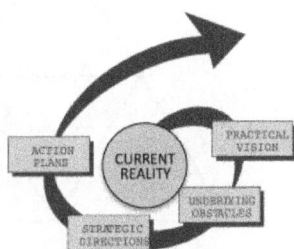

Current Reality: provocative questions that grounds participants.
Practical Vision: formed rapidly from as many people as possible
Underlying Obstacles: pushed until the group says "Ah Ha!"
Strategic Directions: formed out of the consensus of the group
Action Plans: rapidly formed by volunteer teams with passion.

This is done indoors or outdoors, with big groups or small, using writing and or drawings, bi-lingually or in one language. With good training, a community will pick up on this, and add their own touch. Sure, there is a 110 page manual, but for village people, they pick up the process fairly quickly, and use what works for them. ICA has trained over 30,000 in this method, and their probably someone close to you that is well trained.

The Social Process Triangles

We use the Social Process to keep the group's attention inclusive when doing a vision session by focusing on gaining balance, and often plotting their vision-ideas on large charts distributed around the group. We did this with a community of 350 people in Mexico and they were so eager to see the results, and many places as well. It never fails to provide amazing results, even when the community has a focused need like water and food and education.

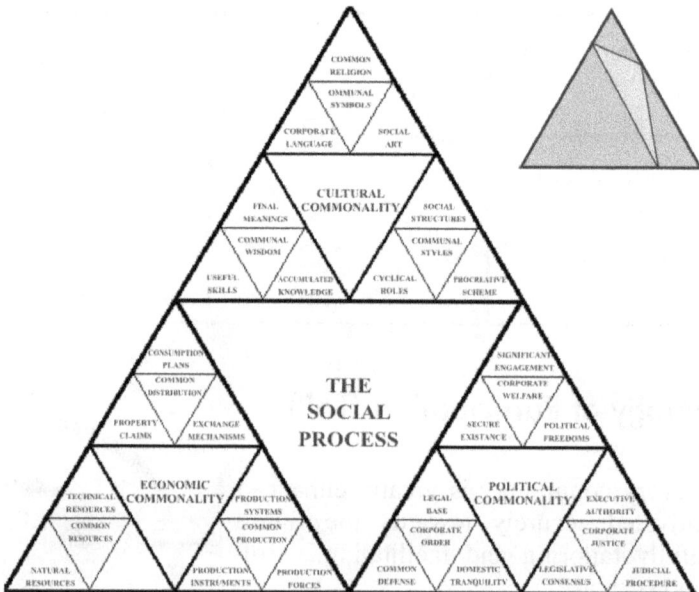

Processes for Sustainable Community Development

Careful attention must be placed on Process in the community. Here is a
list Pune and Japan compiled, but it is mixed with processes and activities:

Process Leadership for Sustainable Community Development

- Authorization Visits
- Vocational Training
- Leadership Training
- Self-Esteem Training
- Building Social Capital (any way you can do it) (in Kosuge Mura, we
  brought city youth to village and picked trash much to the surprise of
  villagers)
- Frequent checking with each other
- Quarterly Reviews
- Be regularly in the community
- Use "short courses" every chance
- Community "Work Days"
- New Festivals – (Pune combined normal festival with Environmental
  Focus)
- Focused Action Plans
- In-formal Schooling
- Health Camps = Health Checkup Days
- Sports Days
- Exchange Programs
- ICA Training in the Community
- "Rights" and "Responsibilities" Dialogues
- Focused Conversations on Issues of Concern
- Secular Spirit Training
- Technical Input
- Micro Credit Systems
- Training on Social Process Triangle (Promotes Balanced Development
  at all levels)
- Training about the Programmatic Chart (Promotes Inclusive Concerns)

- Early Childhood Education (include the Learning Basket)
- Dignitary Visits
- Values Discussions – local and international perspectives
- Engaging the government
- Building a model for replication
- Environmental Education
- Field Trips
- International Exchanges.

Process of Participatory Community Development – ICA Peru

Here is an example of thinking "process", with the development principles built in, used by ICA Peru, after ICA Japan worked with them providing Emergency Aid after the Chincha Earthquake:

Leadership Invitation. ICA-Peru works in a community starts with soliciting the permission of the established leadership to receive an overview of community needs and an official invitation to work with the community in meeting those needs.

Resident Input. The participatory process begins with direct contact with the residents, preferably with a structured community workshop which generates a written document, but at minimum with many informal meetings in homes, workplaces and on the streets. In the case of the Chincha Alta earthquake, the meetings were in the streets and the unmet needs were stated as food and shelter.

Geographic Sectors. Once the key need is selected, the geographic area to be served is divided into 20 to 30 sectors of several blocks each, such that the need is balanced in each of those sectors. In Chincha Alta, the focus was on building temporary houses, so the 30 sectors were drawn on the map to include about 50 families in each sector who needed housing. It is critical that ALL families in the target geography are included in a sector, whether they need assistance or not.

Promoters Selected. For each sector, the families or that sector are requested to select two Promoters to be trained to be the leaders of the Project in their sector. The families are given a sheet of guidelines for being a Promoter, but the ICA has absolutely nothing to do with the selection process, and never makes any effort to make a judgment in the selection process. This assures that the Promoters are truly representatives of the

people of each sector and not of the ICA. An orientation meeting is held
for all of the Promoters one week before the bus leaves for the Promoter
training. This gives people time to prepare, and for a few, the opportunity
to change their minds and be replaced by another who is willing to take
on the responsibility. The 60 Promoters are trained in two groups of 30 to
keep it intimate.

Promoters Trained. The first 30 Promoters meet in the central plaza
on a Sunday afternoon to leave for five days of training at the ICA
Training Center in Azpitia, about 2 hours from Chincha. The Center is
fully residential with excellent training facilities and access to all of the
exciting changes that have occurred in the demonstration community of
Azpitia over the past 28 years. The training focuses on personal growth
and confidence in order to awaken the leadership skills in the Promoters.
They are also given the practical experience of organizing and doing a
workday and a celebration, as well as practical sessions on the details of
building the houses. After five days of learning and working together they
are closely bonded as a team. The following week, the other 30 Promoters
go through the same training.

Sector Models Built. After meeting to receive their tools, each group of
30 Promoters builds a highly visible model house for the whole community,
followed by a model house in each of their 15 sectors. These 15 houses
are completed in the first week of work, creating an incredible amount of
excitement throughout the community, and a huge amount of energy to
move the Project forward. The ICA staff is careful to not be accessible
for consultation on the methods and quality of the construction in order
to assure that the Promoters continue to learn to work as leaders who are
totally in charge of the Project. However, the staff observes closely and
makes comments if necessary to remind the Promoters of certain details
they may have overlooked. The ICA staff are consultants, not directors of
the Project.

Family Work Teams. Now each pair of Promoters is ready to organize
their entire sector into work teams of five families each. These teams are
expected to work together to cooperatively build each of their five houses,
which gives support to families who may not have the physical ability
to do the work unassisted on their own house. In communities where
there are many seniors and single mothers this is a very important part of
the process. Of course, this has an important side effect of binding the
community together to assist in other aspects of rebuilding.

Completion Incentive. The teams are required to complete, within one week, the construction of the houses for all five families. As an incentive, they receive the delivery of the fine wooden doors for their houses ONLY when all five houses are completed. Finally, the ICA staff makes an inspection of each house and places a sticker on the door, a sign that the house meets the quality standards of the Project. The stickers have become a much sought-after sign of quality and completion.

Community Spirit. While the ICA staff is in almost daily contact with the Promoters, the staff holds a meeting with the Promoters every two weeks during the Project implementation to maintain the unity of the team and to make any corrections in the direction of the Project. These events are lively and fun and every one of them has some element of future vision for the community. While the ICA does not make any direct suggestions on other actions the Promoters might take to improve their community, the results of these events has been an out-pouring of spirit that has shown up in neighborhood banners, community clean-up efforts, spontaneous workdays, and even a neighborhood Christmas decoration competition between residents of the new houses. In fact, a new community is being created.

Closing Celebration. At the end of the three months of work on the Project, the Promoters organize a grand celebration for themselves with some small assistance from the ICA staff. In effect, it is a thank you celebration for the assistance of the ICA to their community. The bonds which were created in this way have lasted and turned into many ongoing relationships of assistance in the subsequent work of the ICA in the community.

Technology of Spirit

I sometimes am faced with setbacks or other re-occurring problems, either with projects or individuals. Last year, I began asking:

Why do relationships often end up with the same negative outcome?

Why you are unable to change your destructive behavior?

How do we find inner peace in the midst of chaos?

How and why does your belief systems limit your potential?

How does one clear up blocks, obsessions, habitual behavior and emotional limitations?

Why do some projects or activities fail soon after one leaves, even after extensive training?

Why is it often difficult to move communities to inclusive awareness?

One extensive method works to identify, clear, and replace programs or patterns from this life and past lives, and reprograms your life with love, joy, and spiritual purpose. Emerging in the 21st Century are technologies which are new components that complete our set of renewal technologies, without which we will forever be limited in our efforts to create a peaceful planet on which to have a heavenly life.

Most communities are deprived of one thing or another – In a learning community, that is why they incarnated on Earth at this time.

Most individuals and communities have blocks that are carried forward from their inherited past, and can be cleared with Spirit Technologies, so that they can actually go forward freely with ToC and ToP. Yes, we are for the first time broadly aware of spirit technologies that can clear away past experiences and offer a fresh lease on life with great energy.

ToC & ToP are widely practiced in over 40 countries; I believe the Technology of Spirit is the growing and emerging powerful to be the master technology that is spreading rapidly in the 21st Century.

I may focus on the Technology of Spirit my next 25 years.

Resources are sustaining us on the journey are:
Colleagues from around the world who relate to ICA Japan
The following three book sets which have are extremely valuable, read over and over:
Conversations with God, series of three books Neal Donald Walsh
Power vs Force, by David R. Hawkins
Anastasia, series of nine books by Valdimir Megre (Russian)
And three which are on our horizon:
The Art of Soaring, by Dolokhov & Gurangov
The Power of Luck, by Dolokhov & Gurangov
Soul Re-Creation, Developing Your Cosmic Potential, Robert Detzler.

Conclusion

We have begun to unlock profound thinking and look towards deeper technologies of the Spirit so that we are released from the past, get in synchronization with our Higher Selves, follow the guidance from our hidden intuitions, and from the Universe and SPIRIT itself. Equally important is to learn to release other people and places in the same manner. Only in this way will we achieve our common goal of a truly peaceful world.

This is not new to ICA; we have used our presence, our singing, and our spirit exercises to this end. Now there exists a technology of Spirit which when combined with our other practices we will achieve much more.

Each person finds ways to create space for love in our hearts, to create an environment which opens doors for peace. Some people meditate, some create open space, some work in their garden, some run next to a lake, others work with people in conflict, or create dialogues so that fighting will become less, and yet others listen to their cat purr on their chest. Let's work together to give peace a greater chance.

Please learn another Technology of Spirit right away!

Changing Lives and Changing Societies: Role of ICA in Nepal

Tatwa P. Timsina, PhD and Ishu Subba

With an aim of changing lives and changing societies, Institutes of Cultural Affairs (ICA) Nepal was established in early 1998 in Kathmandu, Nepal. Since its establishment, following its philosophy 'every individual has a capacity to bring change in his/her situation' ICA Nepal is continuously working in human capacity development and hence emerged as one of the leading organizations in training and facilitation in Nepal. ICA Nepal believes that no sustainable change and development is achieved without considering existing cultural dynamics and pluralities. Thus, it is dedicated to create an environment, an opportunity of participation in building sustainable change and development.

In the past 15 years, several changes occurred at local, national and global context. Nepal witnessed decade long insurgency, political upheavals and movement which replaced traditional monarchy system to republic system. During the turmoil of conflict and violence, the presence of government in the villages, local communities; civil organization like ICA Nepal played a remarkable role in making transformation. ICA worked in changing attitudes of warring factions and enhancing public participation for the revival of democracy. Through its small initiation, it has been able to reach thousands of people at various parts of countries.

Since its inception, ICA Nepal is playing significant role in the country to achieve remarkable improvements in terms of people's participation, equality, leadership and improving lives. ICA will continue this role in future and expects to bring a big impact by transforming societies.

Starting ICA in Nepal:

The Institute of Cultural Affairs – Nepal (ICA-N) started working in Nepal from 1996 and was formally established in March 1998 in Kathmandu as an autonomous, non-governmental organisation registered with the Government of Nepal and Social Welfare Council, Nepal.

Globally, the Institute of Cultural Affairs has over five decades of experience of building human capacities through participation, training and facilitation activities and setting up community development programmes. ICA is concerned with the 'human factor in development', strengthening human capabilities in the public, NGO and private sectors.

Since its formal establishment in 1998, ICA-N has grown rapidly, focusing on research, training, facilitation and community development activities. As a strategy, ICA's basic concern is on participation based activities which focus on building human capacities across the cultures, regions and genders.

ICA's mission is to promote social innovation by enhancing participation and community building. ICA Nepal aims to promote a culture of participation at all levels of the society, encourage people and groups to participate in alleviating poverty and discrimination, introduce the experience of other world-wide ICAs into the Nepali context, and empower communities and organisations through facilitation skills.

By 2015, ICA Nepal aims to enlarge opportunities of the disadvantaged communities and ordinary people in Nepal enhancing individual and organisational capacity through training, facilitation and human developmental activities.

History of ICA Nepal:

ICA Nepal's history can be traced back since 1996. In 1996, Dr. Tatwa P. Timisina came in touch with ICA methods and practices while being in Belgium as a student at VUB; where he participated several ICA training and facilitation programs. In the same year, for the very first time, ICA Malaysia organized ToP training in Nepal.

In the following year, on Dr. Timsina's initiation; a group came together and got trained in ICA methods; this led a pave for establishment of ICA in Nepal. In 1998, ICA Nepal was formally registered and in same year, ICA International's Dick Alton facilitated first ToP training in Nepal.

Since, 1999, ICA Nepal introduced its community development activities in ten districts of Nepal; and applied ToP method at local level in Nepal.

"Dalit" (so-called untouchables) empowerment movement was started in Parbat district, which is one of the remarkable achievements of ICA Nepal. In the same year, Eva Harris of Vision Trust supported ICA Nepal for organizational strengthening activities.

With the incredible support from MOFA, Japan and MISEREOR, Germany, in 2001 ICA Nepal started a comprehensive community development projects in western part of Nepal. In 2002, ICA accomplished another project "Decentralized Transformative Approaches Leadership Programme". In the same year, a learning center was established in Changunarayan, Bhaktapur. In 2003, ICA Nepal facilitated to start ICA Bangladesh and ICA International team trained local staffs on ICA methodology. In 2004, Tatwa P. Timsina, elected as the President of ICA International. In 2005, ICA launched Social Artistry Leadership Program in Nepal. With the technical support of CIVICUS, and partial financial support of Action Aid Nepal and IDRC, ICA Nepal released "Civil Society Index". ICA worked as a partner organization of MSH, and ADRA Nepal in Result Oriented Leadership Development Programme supported by USAID in 2006 and ICA trained 300 teachers on life skills based education. ICA implemented CSI recommendations nationally. In 2007, ICA Nepal in partnership with Global Forest Coalition launched an action research work entitle "Underlying Causes of Forest Destruction" in three districts. ICA Nepal implemented an intensive community development project in Far Western Region with the support of Poverty Alleviation Fund, Nepal. Professional Career Development Training (PCDT), a 3 months long training program was started and since 2006 ICA has successfully completed series of PCDT.

2008 is a notable year for ICA. In this year, ICA joined JHF and planned to train 5000 people on SA leadership in Nepal. In partnership with Robertson Work International Fund for Social Artistry and International Institute of Social Artistry, ICA implemented Micro Grants Support to 30 youths. In 7th Global Conference on Human Development, 2008 held in Japan, ICA Nepal proposed to host 8th Global Conference on Human Development in Nepal due to then ongoing change and development taking place in the Nepal.

In 2009, ICA supported the ideas of some facilitators to start ICA Associates and in 2010 worked in developing Masters' Level Curriculum on Training and Development. In 2011, ICA Nepal established Institute of Training and Human Development (ITHD) as a sister organization; which is registered and governed by company rule of Nepal. The only objective of establishing ITHD is to support ICA. ITHD conducts training

194 • Changing Lives, Changing Societies
ICA's Experience in Nepal and in the World

and facilitation courses as a source of income generation.

2012 is another exciting year for ICA Nepal. ICA Nepal is hosting 8th Global Conference on Human Development. The 8th Global Conference will run over 5 days from October 29 to November 2, 2012 and has included 6 major themes which range from leadership, education, peace building, building viable future planet earth to building strategies for comprehensive development and resourcing human development.

Transforming Individuals through Training and Facilitation

Participation matters in every time zone, and in private, public and community setting. ICA has developed set of participatory methods termed as "Technology of Participation" which enable bringing high level of participation to the decision making process which bring change in lives. ToP methods cultivate change, collect ideas, generate the spirit of ownership, create clear goals and open lines of communication, broaden perspectives, and inspire people to adapt to their changing environment.

ICA Nepal has developed itself as a leading organization in training and facilitation. Since its establishment, based on ToP method ICA Nepal is conducting several public and in–house courses. These courses are highly participatory and have brought effective change and result in and among groups, communities. As a public course, ICA Nepal is conducting major four courses which train participants to use four core ToP tools, namely: Focused Group Discussion, the Workshop Method, the Action Planning Method and the Participatory Strategic (PSP) Method.

Transforming Lives through Development Projects:

ICA Nepal believes and follows small initiation can bring an effective change in lives, society and nation. Thus, in the last 15 years, ICA Nepal has successfully implemented several community development projects in various parts of the country. Facilitation and participation approach have remained the zest of all community development activities of ICA Nepal. We start with application of facilitation skills, which allow community people to realize and identify the change; then strategic planning sessions are organized to form a task force with designated responsibilities and time frame for implementing the plan. A micro finance group is formed and ownership is granted to the group to run the program professionally. Series of capacity building trainings and facilitation sessions are conducted to capacitate the community people to run the projects successfully.

The first initiation of ICA Nepal was financially supported by Rabobank Foundation, Netherlands and implemented in Parbat district. The project entitled "Micro-Credit and Saving in Five VDCs of Partbat District" targeted socially, economically marginalized and deprived group "dalit". The project focused on raising the socio-economic status of deprived women of the targeted group through income generation. Two hundred and fifty women received credit and utilized the amount in small scale income generating activities. Women got self-employed and got involved in animal rearing, sewing clothes, etc. Now, the saving group has been transformed to one of the leading cooperatives in dalit communities, probably the first in Nepal.

One of the pioneer works of ICA Nepal is in the field of education especially in adult literacy. With the support of CARITAS Nepal, "Empowering Dalit community in Three VDCs of Parbat District" was successfully implemented. The project concentrated on adult literacy, animation and income generating activities. In coordination of Department of Education, Nepal, ICA carried out Community School Support Project in eleven districts. ICA Nepal, through this project assisted the school management in transforming the school from centrally controlled to community managed school. In this project, activities such as preparing participatory strategic plan, raising awareness of local people about importance of education, providing support to management committee in managing the school systematically and carrying out regular monitoring and evaluation for the teaching effectiveness in the school were carried. In recognition for the contribution of ICA under this project, ICA was honoured as one of the best NGOs in education sector by the Ministry of Education of Nepal.

Three years long "Enhancing and Protecting Interventions Prorgram" was initiated, with a support of Rural Access Program (RAP/DFID). The project activities covered the location of Baneshwor to Khandbaari sector spanning 41 KM under Basantapur Khandbaari Feeder Road Project. The project aimed to create safe and sustainable livelihood condition of poor and disadvantaged people of targeted VDCs in Sankhuwasabha district.

ICA Nepal has been rigorously working in different VDCs of Parbat District implementing a project entitled "Facilitating Participatory Planning and Development for Ethnic Minorities and Lower Caste People in Parbat District of Nepal"; which carried out activities like working on participatory strategic planning, street dramas, and construction of low cost toilets, cook stoves, soakpits, adult literacy, micro credit, gender and development and informal leadership development trainings. With the support of ICA Japan and Association for International Cooperation of Agriculture and Forestry (AICAF), ICA Nepal carried out sustainable agricultural activities in far remote areas of Nepal.

ICA Nepal is continuously working in human development with or without financial support of any donor organization. ICA Nepal is running small scale community development projects through its own source of income. It is generating funds through conducting training and facilitation courses. It is committed to spend 30% of its income generated through training and other activities in community development.

Social Artistry Initiatives in Nepal

After a series of preparatory activities, Social Artistry Initiative was formally launched in Nepal in 2005. At first 55 participants from various districts of Nepal and from Bangladesh participated in the training. It implemented model pilot projects in four different parts of the country representing all three ecological belts i.e., plain (terai), mountain and Himalayan regions. Social Artistry has been implemented as an effective tool for achieving Millennium Development Goals (MDGs) in these areas.

With the support of Jean Houston Foundation (JHF) and International Institute of Social Artistry, ICA Nepal has been conducting social artistry leadership training ranging from one day to 10 days. In support of Robertson Work International Fund for Social Artistry and International Institute of Social Artistry, micro grants support to youth were implemented. The project included such as orientation/training, request for proposal and providing micro grants, implementation of the projects, developing case study (one by each participant), monitoring and reporting and sharing of the success stories. This project was started in May, 2008. In the first phase, the grant was provided to 30 people who have had some experience on social artistry.

Human Capacity Building through Social Artistry

Durga Adhikari, a resident of Devdaha, West Nepal is a local facilitator who looks for innovative solutions to problems of his community. Devdaha is about 200 kilometer far from Kathmandu and is located near the birth place of Buddha.

Durga has passion of lifelong learning and aims for new skills, ideas and insights. He is determined to share his knowledge and skills, and has an aim to create a difference in his community as well as in the world. As a practitioner of Social Artistry, he uses his intellectual, physical, emotional and cultural exploration using whole mind. He has developed a wide range of innate capacities to create innovative solutions to critical issues confronting his communities and societies. He is able to formulate models of change that he uses in a broad range of his society.

ICA Nepal implemented a project on Social Artistry this work with the objectives of developing model learning site with the focus on achieving MDGs locally. It is aimed to carry on regular research and documentation on application of social artistry to achieve MDGs and replicating the success of the project in achieving MDGs locally, nationally and globally.

In the strategic planning workshop, the community underlined poor health facilities, unsafe drinking water, inadequate skill human resources, poor literacy rate, drudgery of women life, poverty as major development challenges in the area. The community designed 10 year long strategic directions to achieve MDGs. They are considered as the roadmap for MDGs at the local context. Local people along with the ICA Nepal designed a program to develop leadership skills among the local community focusing to achieve MDGs.

Local people implemented the plan integrating MDGs and social artistry. The work brought a lot of changes in the area. Within the community, several people were trained directly on various skills such as social artistry, leadership development, income generation etc.

Local community makes their own plan for their comprehensive development. They are implementing various projects which help in minimizing poverty in the area. They have highlighted the importance of physical infrastructure, employment creation, modern agriculture etc for poverty reduction.

Many people in the area are now own small businesses which help them to enhance their economic condition. In the past, majority of the people were below the poverty line, now there is steady increase in local economy. Another major means of poverty alleviation in the area is microfinance activities. Local people believe that there is a need of saving and flow of money in the community. They are able to meet most of the goals of MDGs at local level.

Prepared by Tatwa P. Timsina

Research:

ICA Nepal, in collaboration with Voluntary Service Overseas (VSO) carried out series of workshops. The objective of the workshops was to find partner NGOs in the Far West. Organizational assessment workshops were held in disadvantaged districts. For CARITAS Nepal, ICA Nepal carried out intensive research work using PRA tools and techniques to investigate about the status of women and children in relation to environmental and social aspects. For Rural Access Program (RAP) of DFID, ICA studied the availability of labour force during the implementation of the road project of the Bhojpur and Doti districts. ICA Nepal successfully completed a research work on milk marketing in Far Western Development Region for Third Livestock Development Project (TLDP).

Responsibility for Sustainability

Ms Gita Magar (39) lives in Changunarayan, Gurung Gaon village, Bhaktapur District. She lives with her two children – one daughter (12 years old), a son (15 years old) and her husband. Now she is the president of community drinking water user group.

Before implementation of the Changunarayan Drinking Water Project in her community, Gita used to walk around one hour to Bundhara to fetch water. The way in the jungle was horrifying and the trail was in poor condition. She had to go back three to four times per day which was very difficult specially during her pregnancy and while menstruating.

Now Gita is using water from the point near her house for drinking and other household purposes. She is using waste water in the kitchen garden where she grows tomatoes, onions, beans, cucumbers, pumpkins, maize, spinach and chili. She also knows the rules for purifying drinking water such as boiling, solar disinfection etc. and she is aware of food hygiene – covering cooked food and water buckets. Gita's house is now cleaner which she enjoys sharing with others and using as an example to others in the community.

Now she is happy as she is able to save time as she does not need much time to fetch water. She is using that time in income generation activities. Gita wants to give the credit for that to this project. Gita is also committed to the sustainability of this project.

Prepared by Radha Subedi

Volunteer Program

ICA has already hosted more than 20 international volunteers to various development projects across Nepal. Volunteers often come from USA, Japan, UK and the Netherlands. Volunteering program has benefitted in exchanging and sharing skills and practices for community development. We have three types of volunteering programmes including Volunteering Support Program, Internship and Study Tour.

Publications

ICA has published a number of publications on Proposal Writing and Fundraising, ToT and Facilitation, Social Style, Participatory Monitoring and Evaluation (PPME), Financial Service Association, Winning through Participation, Participatory Rural Appraisal, Group Mobilisation and Dynamics, Civil Society in Nepal, Manual on Training of Trainers, Manual on Project Proposal Writing and Fund Raising, Bio Diversity, Manual on Leadership and Management etc.

Conclusion

ICA has been continuously working for comprehensive human development and capacity building. Through its continuous initiation and effort, ICA is trying to reach rural remote community people. ICA methods are applied sincerely to bring positive change in disadvantaged, marginalized communities with high commitment in human development.

About the Authors

Ana Mari Urrutia, was Executive Manager at the Instituto de Rehabilitación Infantil (an institution dedicated to help Physically Challenged children) from 1973 to 1995. Since 1997 she is Executive Secretary of the Board of the Sociedad Pro-Ayuda al Niño Lisiado, that's in charge of the Institution. She is a specialist in Participation Technology, trained at the Institute of Cultural Affairs in Chicago (1984) and in Phoenix, Arizona (1995-96). She is now Trainer and part of the board of ICA Chile (Secretary). Her personal e- mail is anamariurrutia@yahoo.es.

Azizur Rahman, Assistant Professor of Mawlana Bhashani Science and Technology University, is the founder of ICA in Bangladesh. He is currently pursuing a PhD in criminology at the University of Ottawa, following an MA in criminology from the University of Toronto, holding honours degree in sociology, and two other master's degrees in sociology, and regional development planning. He has long been engaged in multidisciplinary research, teaching, and human development work at home and abroad. Aziz has been honoured with a number of prestigious awards and grants including German Academic Exchange Service (DAAD) Fellowship, University of Toronto Fellowship, University of Ottawa Excellence Scholarship, and Social Science Research Council (SSRC) Promotional research grant. He has also worked with a number of other reputed organizations like Bangladesh Institute of Development Studies, Bangladesh Consultants Limited (BCL), Centre for Criminological Research Bangladesh, and International Centre for the Prevention of Crime (ICPC).

Bill Staples is a principal of ICA Associates Inc., a facilitation and training firm whose mission is to create a culture of participation in every sector of society and to provide core funding to the charitable work of ICA. Bill provides government departments, companies, civil society and municipalities with facilitation expertise in strategic planning, public consultation, work group implementation and conferences, and trains hundreds of people each year in ToP methods. Bill is the publisher of Group Facilitation: A Research and Applications Journal of the International Association of Facilitators, and was the founding publisher of Edges: New Planetary Patterns. He is very active in international volunteer work with the ICA global network, and lives in Toronto within walking distance of the office, with his wife Ilona.

Catalina Quiroz Niño, Technology of Participation (ToP) international trainer and facilitator. Training, facilitation and research coordinator and consultant of the Institute of Cultural Affairs in Spain and Empower Training & Development, CIC (Community Interest Company), United Kingdom. Visiting Fellow of York St. John University, United Kingdom and Associate Teacher to the Spanish Open University, Spain.

Dasarath Neupane, a MA & M Phil in English, is an English language teacher as well as a trainer. He has been teaching in schools and colleges from 20 years. He has also good platform in academic research. Recently, he is a Ph D scholar from Dr. K.N. Modi University, India. His research area is in School Bullying in Nepal.

Isabel de la Maza graduated as Teacher in History and Geography at the Catholic University of Chile. She has a vast experience working in social development in Northern Chile and in Central-America as a co-ordinator of intercultural social projects. Isabel worked with the aymara culture during 1985 until 1999 using her knowledge of participation methods learned at the Institute of Cultural Affairs. At the same time, she specialises in gender perspectives related to the development, design and evaluation of social projects. In 1999, through a scholarship granted by the United Nations Programme, she assisted to intensive courses delivered by the Institute of Cultural Affairs in Phoenix, Arizona. Now she trains others in these matters, specially physically challenged people. Actually she is the Executive Director of ICA Chile, and a member of Global Leadership Team, Her email is isadelamaza@gmail.com

Ishu Subba is a post graduate in Sociology with four years of work experience in the development sectors especially in training, facilitation coordination. In this short duration, Ishu has unearthed her inherent skills in organizing seminars, conferences and other events. Energetic in her dealings, she has put herself fully into her work and taken utmost care in completing each task with perfection. She served as consultant in South

Asia Technical Support Facility for HIV, where she supported the program staff with consultant database management, consultant search. Her major work experiences include program officer in ICA Associates where she coordinated development training, and assisted in proposal writing and fund raising. Since March, 2010 she is teaching students at the Master's and Bachelor's level at three colleges in Kathmandu – Sagarmatha Multiple College, Campion College and Nobel College. Currently, Program Manager at ICA Nepal and is working as Conference Secretary for 8th Global Conference on Human Development, 2012.

Janet Sanders works as the principle of PEOPLEnergy, an organisation offering leadership courses, consultancy, strategic planning and global transformation education to fulfill the human factor in development. At the time of the Project, Janet was a consultant for the UNDP on decentralising the Millennium Development Goals. Janet has been staff and volunteer with various ICAs all over the world. She is also one of the leading trainers on social artistry at Jean Houston Foundation, USA.

Jonathan Dudding has worked with the Institute of Cultural Affairs for twenty years, working primarily in Europe, Africa and more recently in the Middle East. Now based in London and Director of International Programmes at ICA:UK, Jonathan's work focuses on the international development sector, providing training (in ToP methods), facilitation services and consultancy to national and international development agencies and working closely with partner organisations in Africa to support their development and growth. Since 2006 working with conflict has assumed greater significance in Jonathan's work, through his involvement with the Kumi project in Israel and Palestine.

Ken Hamje is currently Executive Director of ICA Peru. Ken has a MS in Economics and got an education in the global economy working for four multi-national companies before joining the Institute of Cultural Affairs in 1969 in Chicago with a determination to find a way to build viable local alternatives to the dominance of global interests. After experience with the ICA's integral community development methods in 24 nations, Ken settled in Peru in 1982 to facilitate the building of a viable demonstration community that could be replicated across the country. Now he coaches a skilled Peruvian staff of 15 who form hundreds of new volunteer community leaders every year to apply tested models in developing their communities and local economies without dependence on outside expert assistance or funding. After the 8.0 Chincha earthquake in 2007, the ICA staff used these same local initiative methods in the recovery with dramatic results. More recently, the Peru staff has been called upon to use ICA's community self-development approach to serve in some of the most conflictive zones of natural resource extraction, enabling the local people to take creative control of the destiny of their communities.

Ken engages his passion for local autonomy through research, teaching and writing about facilitation methods for consensus-guided development of local economies which create viable communities for 21st century living.

Kushendra Bahadur Mahat, Executive Director of ICA Nepal has experience of more than 24 years of working in various organizations in Nepal. He enjoys developing the policies and guidelines and management of Finance, Administration, Human Resource and Institutional Development of the organizations.

He has performed as an Executive Director of Karnali Integrated Rural Development and Research Center (KIRDARC) for 6 years and as Finance and Administration Manager of Oxfam GB and Head of Account of Nepal Water for Health, NEWAH for 10 years. He also holds the position of Chairperson and Managing Director in few business companies including schools, college, IT Company, training centre, tour and trekking etc. At present he is pursuing PhD in Management from Dr. K. N. Modi University in India.

Lawrence Philbrook is currently the Executive Director of ICA Taiwan and the President of ICA International. Lawrence joined the Institute of Cultural Affairs in 1972 in the US and has worked internationally since 1977 doing extensive work in over 25 nations. For the past 22 years he has been based in Taiwan while working across Asia.

After leaving the US, his first ten years focused on initiating effective development partnerships with rural communities in Africa and Asia. Beginning in 1985 Mr. Philbrook began facilitating private sector groups as well developing leadership and ongoing organizational change.

For the last 30 years his key skill is in working across all sectors to do collaborative design and facilitation of processes which help to recover a sense of respect and trust as a basis for establishing organizations that can learn and change. His clients include communities, multinational and local companies, NGO's as well as the United Nations and local government organizations. Lawrence Philbrook, Certified ToP Facilitator is also the Director, Institute of Cultural Affairs.

Luz Marina Aponte Gálvez, International facilitator in Strategic Planning and Effective Leadership. Family coach and facilitator for the Parents´ programme: "How to be better parents", "Sexual Education for our kids", "Assertivity". Teacher specializing in speech, language and learning. Currently, Coordinator and Teacher of the Peruvian Educational Programme "Corazón de María", that caters for pupils with attention deficit disorder and behavioural problems. Member of ICA Spain and faculty member of Empower Training & Development, CIC (Community Interest Company), United Kingdom.

Md. Mohsin Ali is a research associate of ICA Bangladesh. He had his honours and master's degrees in English from the University of Dhaka. He had another master's degree in English Language Teaching. He is presently pursuing a third master's degree in Education at the University of Ottawa. He taught English language and literature for fifteen years at college levels in Bangladesh.

Richard Sims works as the principle of PEOPLEnergy, an organisation offering leadership courses, consultancy, strategic planning and global transformation education to fulfill the human factor in development. Richard was involved as co-facilitator in the project of HIV and AIDS launched in Nepal. Richard has been staff and volunteer with various ICAs all over the world.

Robertson Work is human development practitioner with 42 years experience in 55 countries. Currently New York University professor, director of Innovative Leadership Services, consultant to the UN, the East-West Center and the Fulbright Program and a Fellow of the NYU Research Center on Leadership in Action. Formerly UNDP Principal Policy Advisor in Decentralized Governance for 16 years and senior staff member of the Institute of Cultural Affairs for 21 years, living in the USA, Malaysia, Republic of Korea, Jamaica and Venezuela.

Terry Bergdall lived and worked in Africa for eighteen years from 1984 to 2001. He served for five years as co-director of the Institute of Cultural

Affairs in Kenya where he was responsible for a national program of self-reliant village development. He joined the Swedish Cooperative Centre in 1989 and became the project coordinator for the "Methods for Active Participation Research and Development Project" (MAP) in Zambia, Kenya, and Tanzania. From 1993 to 1996, he served as team leader in Ethiopia for the "Community Empowerment Program," a bi-lateral program funded by the Swedish government. He earned his PhD at the University of Wales with research on participatory evaluation to enhance learning among all stakeholders. He currently resides in Chicago where he serves as the executive director of ICA-USA. He is also an adjunct faculty member of the "Asset Based Community Development" (ABCD) Institute at Northwestern University where an earlier version of this article first appeared.

Tatwa P. Timsina, PhD is associated with Tribhuvan University for the last 24 years as Associate Professor. He is associated with a number of academic institutes in Nepal as teacher to board member. He did Masters in Human Ecology from VUB, Belgium in 1997 and PhD in Education from Kathmandu University in 2008. He has supervised dozens of PhD Students in Nepal for their dissertation work. Apart from teaching, he is actively involved in social development activities through ICA, Rotary Club etc. He was the President of ICA International from 2004-06.

Dr. Timsina also works as a trainer/facilitator for a number of organizations including the Government of Nepal, UNDP, USAID, ADB etc. He facilitates training on various themes such as environmental management, strategic planning, development issues etc. Dr. Timsina has written several books on training and facilitation, environment and development issues. He is also actively involved in Rotary movement in Nepal. He was the President of Rotary Club of Rudramati, Kathmandu in 2008/09. In his active involvement and with the support of many national and international donors, about 10 000 people have received training on various themes and more than 50 community development projects have been implemented in various parts of Nepal.

Wayne Ellsworth, Born in Ohio, USA, grew up in small towns in NW Ohio, and graduated from Blume High School as the Valavictorium. Graduated from Ohio University with a BSEE and a minor in Philosophy in 1962. Employed by IBM for 10 years as a Systems Analyst in Endicott, New York and joined ICA in Chicago in 1972 and helped to create LENS which later became ToP. Marketed LENS across North America, with highlights of facilitating for McDonalds Corp, the State government of Minnesota, and Eatons Department Store in Vancouver. Attended Summer Researh Programs of ICA from 1972 to 1984. Went to Frankfurt Germany and worked with the Frankfurt and Brussels ICA office Went to ICA Japan the Spring of 1986, married Shizuyo Sato, facilitated LENS across Japan, and established International Programs and Training Centers Worked in over 20 countries, with emphasis on India, Nepal, Peru, Chile, Brazil, The Philippines, Kenya, and Japan Read Conversations with God, Power vs Force, Anastasia, The Art of Soaring, The Power of Luck, and took courses in the Technology of Spirit, and Professionally Facilitating the Technology of Spirit, The Technology of Participation, and The Technology of Community. In the Summer of 2012 went on a one month retreat and discerned the future path of Society and where ICA Japan will create 16 Profound Centers to bring about the New Society and the New Universe.

Addresses of ICA

INTERNATIONAL SECRETARIAT

C/O ICA Canada,
655 Queen Street East
Toronto, ON. M4M 1G4
Canada
t +1.416.691.2316
f +1.416.691.2491
icai@ica-international.org

STATUTORY MEMBERS

ICA AUSTRALIA
Ray Richmond
Public Officer
6/53 Shore Street East,
Cleveland, 4163
Australia
t/f +61.7.3488.2300
richmonder@iinet.net.au
www.ica-australia.org

ICA BANGLADESH
Mohammed Azizur Rahman
Executive Director (Honorary)
GPO Box 972, Dhaka 1000
Bangladesh. or
Postmaster Lodge, Professor
Para Chandpur-3600,
Bangladesh
t +880.6668242930/841.65719
f +880.2.9001291/8322799
aziz@ica-bangladesh.org
www.ica-banlgladesh.org

ICA BELGIUM
Jim Campbell and Anna A.
Stanley
Rue Amédée Lynen 8,1210
Brussels, Belgium
t +32.2.2190087
f +32.2.2190406
ica.programme@icab.be
www.icab.be

ICA BOSNIA & HERZEGOVINA /BOSPO
Ms. Melika H.Ibrahimbegovi ć
Executive Director
Mirze Delibašića br.9, Tuzla,
B&H,
75000, Tuzia,
Bosnia & Herzegovina
t/f: +387.35.364.330
bospo@bospo.ba
www.bospo.ba

ICA CANADA
Nan Hudson
Executive Director
655 Queen Street East, Toronto
Ontario, Canada M4M 1G4
t +1.416.691.2316
f +1.416.691.2491
ica@icacan.ca
www.icacan.ca

ICA CHILE
Isabel de la Maza
Holanda 1595 Depto. 501,
Providencia, Santiago,
Chile
t +56.2.204.8527
icachile@entelchile.net
www.icachile.cl

ICA COTE D`IVOIRE
Eugene Kouame
Executive Director
BP 3970 Abidjan 01, BP 119,
Brobo,
Côte d'Ivoire
t: +225.04.48.35.23/ 47.26.39.90
cotedivoireica@yahoo.fr
www.ica/international.org/
cotedivoire

ICA INDIA
Shankar Jadhav
Executive Director
Utkarsh, B.T.
Kawade Road, S. No. 46/6

Pawar Baug, Mundhwa,
411036 Pune, India
t +91.2114.226593
icaiindia@vsnl.net
shankarjadhav@icaindiapn.org
http://icaindiapn.org/

ICA JAPAN
Shizuyo Sato
Executive Director
Soshigaya 4-1-22 2F, Setagaya-ku,
Tokyo 157-0072,
Japan
t +81.3.3484.5092
f +81.3.3484.1909
staff@icajapan.org
www.icajapan.org

ICA KENYA
Edward Mutiso
Executive Director
PO Box 21679, Nairobi,
Kenya
t + 254.726.375222
icakenya@ymail.com
www.icakenya.org

ICA MIDDLE EAST and NORTH AFRICA
Sabah Khalifa
Regional Director
119, Misr Helwan Road, Karnak
Building, 4th floor, PB 11431
Maadi, Cairo, Egypt

t 202-5254145 /202-5254118
f 202-5254145
s_khalifa2003@yahoo.com

ICA NEPAL
Tatwa P. Timsina
Chairman
Babarmahal, PO Box 20771,
Kathmandu,
Nepal
t +977.1.4220450/4224145
ica@icanep.wlink.com.np
www.ica-nepal.org

ICA PERU
Kenneth H. L. Hamje
Executive Director
28 de Julio 432,
Magdalena del Mar
Lima 17,
Perú
tf: +511.461.0813
kenh@ica-peru.org
www.ica-peru.org

ICA EHIO (TAJIKISTAN)
Marina Safarova
Executive Director
13 Microdistrict, House 67, Apt 19
735700 Khujand City, Sogh Oblast
Tajikistan
t +992.3422.278.55
ica_ehio@yahoo.ca

www.ica-international.org/
tajikistan

ICA TAIWAN
Gail West
Director
3/f, No.12, Lane 5, Tien Mou
West Road, Taipei, Taiwan
t +886.2.2871.3150
f +886.2.2871.2870
icataiw@ms69.hinet.net
www.icatw.com

ICA TANZANIA
Doris Mutashobya
Executive Director
PO Box 1016, Moshi,
Kilimanjaro,
Tanzania
t +255.27.275.1000
f +255.784.592970
ica.tanzania@gmail.com
www.ica-international.org/
tanzania

ICA UGANDA
Charles Wabwire
Executive Director
PO Box 70, Kyambogo,
Uganda
t +256.772.429.750
c_wabwire@yahoo.com
www.ica-international.org/uganda

ICA USA

Terry Bergdall
Chief Executive Officer
4750 North Sheridan Road,
Chicago, IL 60640, USA
t +1.773.769.6363
f +1.773.769.1144
chicago@ica-usa.org
www.ica-usa.org

ICA ZIMBABWE

Gerald Gomani
Executive Director
9 Weale Road,
Milton Park,
Harare, Zimbabwe.

or
PO Box CY905, Causeway
tf +263 4 778381
icazim@africaonline.co.zw
www.ica-international.org/
zimbabwe

ICA Sri Lanka

ICA Ukraine

ICA Guatemala

ICA Brazil

ASSOCIATE MEMBERS

LENS International (Malaysia)

John and Anne Epps
Box 10564, 50718 Kuala Lumpur,
Malaysia
t +603.795.75604
f +603.795.64420
annepps@pd.jaring.my
www.lensinternational.com

ICA ZAMBIA OPAD

*OPAD - Organisation for the
Promotion of meaningful
Development through active
Participation*
Voice Vingo
Buchi Road, Northmead
Lusaka 10101 Zambia
voice.vingo@opadzambia.com
www.ica-international.org/zambia

www.ingramcontent.com/pod-product-compliance
Lightning Source LLC
Chambersburg PA
CBHW031507270326
41930CB00006B/298